THE TRIUMPH OF AN IDEA

HENRY FORD

THE
TRIUMPH OF AN IDEA
THE STORY OF HENRY FORD

By
Ralph H. Graves

ILLUSTRATIONS FROM PHOTOGRAPHS

Garden City, New York
Doubleday, Doran & Company, Inc.
1935

PRINTED AT THE *Country Life Press*, GARDEN CITY, N. Y., U. S. A.

CONTENTS

THE TRIUMPH OF AN IDEA

I

A LONE PIONEER

HALF A CENTURY HAS PASSED since Henry Ford's attention was attracted to a contrivance called "a silent gas engine." A German named Otto was the inventor, and a description of the primitive affair in an English magazine caught the eye of the Michigan farm boy, who had now become a machinist in Detroit. He got a chance to repair an Otto engine at the Eagle Iron Works in 1885. The dissection of that single-cylinder machine, run by illuminating gas, marked the start of patient investigations which were to launch the era of motor transport. It marked, also, the beginning of the fifty years which we of today appraise as the period most productive of scientific achievement in the world's history.

Along with the gasoline engine, the automobile and good roads, our generation has seen the conquest of the air, the development of radio and motion pictures, the increase of safeguards for sea travel, the perfection of farming machinery, the upheaval of autocratic governments, and, perhaps most important of all, the spread of education through which the minds and hearts of men are diverted into new channels of thought and feeling. Progress in invention and industry has withstood wars and panics, has defied the periodic hysterias afflicting humanity in their wake.

In the foreground of this progress has evolved the Ford idea, at first an enthusiast's dream in a scoffing world, slowly proving its soundness by years of painstaking research, growing into a vast manufacturing structure, and finally typifying the motor age as a corner stone of our modern industrial system.

Looking backward to the year 1885, one finds it difficult to realize the changes that have come about in the half century. Kings then ruled by "divine right" over a large portion of the earth. Queen Victoria was in her forty-eighth year on the British throne, Alexander III had been Russia's czar for half a decade, a Manchu emperor reigned in China, the Hapsburgs overlorded Austria, Wilhelm II had yet three years to fret before becoming the German Kaiser. In the United States the first term of President Grover Cleveland was just beginning. General U. S. Grant died in that summer. Franklin D. Roosevelt was three years old, Benito Mussolini a year younger. P. T. Barnum was running "the Greatest Show on Earth." The Nestor of the stage was Edwin Booth, and among the bright stars were Lester Wallack, Sir Henry Irving, Joseph Jefferson, Sarah Bernhardt, Helena Modjeska, William H. Crane, and John Drew, while the younger actors behind the footlights included Richard Mansfield, Ada Rehan, Eleonora Duse, Kate Claxton, and Lily Langtry.

Hadfield's invention of manganese steel and Parsons's steam turbine were the wonders of the past twelvemonth. Only sixteen years earlier the last spike of the first transcontinental railway had been driven into a Utah desert, and twenty-one years had gone since the development of the open-hearth process, the birth of the age of steel.

The incandescent electric light was but six years old. For household and street lighting, illuminating gas had been one of the wonders of modern ingenuity until Thomas A. Edison, in 1879, completed the long series of experiments which resulted in his vacuum bulb containing a filament that emitted, when electrified, a light brighter and more serviceable than any hitherto known. Edison's interminably careful methods were exemplified by this most famous of his inventions. He spent years trying out materials for a filament, discarding platinum because of its cost, and almost abandoning carbon because it blew itself to pieces if electrified in contact with air. On discovering that the carbon would burn in a vacuum without destroying itself, he had the problem well-nigh solved. There yet remained a vast amount of detail, however, before perfection could be reached. Hundreds of materials were used for filament before the inventor decided that bamboo was the best. Thereupon he sent men all over the world to find the most superior bamboo. The Japanese variety was chosen after the search had cost $100,000. For years that fiber was used satisfactorily, until it was supplanted by a more economical filament made by squirting a solution of cellulose through glass jets into alcohol. When the alcohol coagulates, the hardened cellulose is carbonized by heat. There can be no doubt that prior to the motor age Edison's incandescent lamp was the invention which most vitally affected the everyday life of the everyday man.

In the autumn of 1885 the first electric street railway

in the United States was opened in Baltimore. Even this visible marvel in transportation was regarded by the public as an achievement of limited possibilities. The idea that a horseless vehicle with no tracks beneath it would ever travel over the open road was too much for the imagination of all save a few dreamers. The "horseless carriage," of which visionaries had talked for hundreds of years, was still as distant, so far as the average man could see, as it had been when Leonardo da Vinci invented the wheelbarrow.

But Henry Ford and the other creative scientists of the day were not average men. In Ford's mind the engine that would be strong enough and light enough to propel a vehicle for passengers or freight was imminent. He was not the only inventor who worked toward the goal; but he was a lone pioneer, for only in the vaguest way did he know what the others were doing in the early stages of his experiments. Of course, as he learned in later years about the discoveries of chemists and mechanics here and abroad, he studied their findings, accepted the principles that proved valuable, and rejected ideas that failed to accord with his own conclusions. He gave credit where credit was due, never hesitating to acknowledge the achievement of a competitor. That he succeeded beyond his rivals was due to an open mind as well as to untiring persistence.

When Ford began to tinker with the Otto engine, not a yard of good road, as we understand the term today, had been laid in America. Desultory efforts to improve city streets included the building of a short asphalted pavement in Newark, N. J., in 1870. Two years afterward a brick surface was used in Charleston,

W. Va., and in 1879 a part of Pennsylvania Avenue, in Washington, D. C., was bedded with asphalt. Bicyclists became vocal in their demand for better roads in 1880, but in the ensuing decade the public officials who

Henry Ford as a youth.

interested themselves in road improvements were rarities. The subject was regarded with the same skepticism which greeted any other innovation. It was not until 1892 that modern concrete was used for one side of a square in Bellefontaine, Ohio, and only in 1908 was the first mile of rural concrete built in Wayne County, Michigan. Incidentally, Henry Ford was a member of the county's Board of Road Commissioners in 1906–07.

But that is getting ahead of our story. When Ford

Birthplace of Henry Ford, Dearborn, Michigan.

developed his first definite plan of building an automobile, he thought of a car which would run on the rough roads of Detroit and its vicinity. If he visioned a six-lane concrete highway, he was dreaming as far into the future as Jules Verne dreamed when he forecast the undersea boat.

The idea of gas engines was old, but Otto's effort to put one on the market was the first sign that anybody considered them of practical use. Ford studied the contraption at odd moments in the next two years, mostly at night in his home shop, when he had finished a day's work on his regular job. He read everything within reach on scientific topics, including the tale of Gottlieb Daimler's petroleum-burning engine which was attached to a bicycle, causing great astonishment among the inhabitants of Mannheim, Germany. Doubtless he scanned, without much attention, the newspaper columns of 1886 chronicling the Chicago anarchist riots, Steve Brodie's leap from the Brooklyn Bridge, the Charleston earthquake, and the unveiling of the Statue of Liberty in New York harbor, and in the next year the theater fires of Paris and Exeter with their hundreds of victims, and the drowning of nearly a million Chinese in the Hoang-ho River floods. It is not recorded whether he heard until afterward that Panhard and Levassor bought the French rights of Daimler's invention and in 1887 actually built a motorcar, which was an object of mirth rather than serious interest among the Parisians.

About the time this equipage was clattering over the boulevards, Ford built an engine on the Otto four-cylinder plan, with a one-inch bore and a three-inch stroke, operated by gasoline, and somewhat lighter in weight than the original. Soon afterward he returned to his father's farm, rigged up a workshop for further experiments, and married Miss Clara J. Bryant. They began their life together in a small cottage, a few months before his twenty-fifth birthday, in 1888. When he was not cutting timber, he worked on gas engines.

In the year 1888 the first pneumatic tire was produced by Dunlap, and New York had its famous March blizzard, which could not have held much interest to the young inventor, reared in a region of heavy snows. Probably he gave not a thought to the tragedy of the Austrian Crown Prince Rudolph, whose death by suicide or murder has been a historic puzzle from that day to this. Certainly he did not know that the next year, 1889, was distinguished by the birth of Richard E. Byrd, explorer and flyer, though he may have given passing notice to the inauguration of President Benjamin Harrison, the Johnstown flood, the opening of Oklahoma for settlement, and the admission of four new states: the Dakotas, Washington, and Montana. In 1890 he started to construct a double-cylinder engine, after having built various experimental engines, and decided that for transportation a single-cylinder was impracticable because its flywheel weighed too much.

At first he planned to put the double-cylinder engine on a bicycle, but figured out that with the gas tank and necessary controls it was too heavy. Moving his workshop to the shed in the backyard of a modest city house, when he accepted a $45-a-month job as engineer and machinist with the Edison Illuminating Company of Detroit, he continued experimenting in his "leisure" hours. He has said that in the years of testing and planning he was never doubtful of succeeding, and that his young wife was even more confident in the future of the gasoline-driven automobile. He called her "The Believer."

In the two-year interval before he completed his first car, minor inventions pointing toward the automobile were reported, but none that appreciably influenced

Ford's activities. He stuck to his last and knew little of what was happening outside his daily routine. In the year 1890 the new states of Idaho and Wyoming were admitted into the Union, the People's party held its first

WHERE THE FIRST FORD CAR WAS BUILT
Brick workshop in the inventor's backyard, Bagley Avenue, Detroit, now in the historical village at Dearborn.

convention in Kansas City, the McKinley tariff law went into effect, Chief Sitting Bull was killed in the Sioux war, and the Kingdom of the Netherlands acquired a ten-year-old queen, Wilhelmina. In 1891 a bomb thrower blew himself to pieces when trying to kill Russell Sage in New York, and his identity as a New

Englander named Norcross was established through a button, the only whole thing left intact about him after the explosion. Another happening of that year was New Jersey's establishment of the first Highway Department in the country.

Random discussions of good roads had gained sufficient headway by this time to attract the attention of railway operators. One rail executive was quoted as declining to deliver material to a road contractor on the ground that he did not wish to encourage such competition. Perhaps he had just heard that in 1892 the Massachusetts Legislature voted to initiate the country's second Highway Department, an example soon followed by six other states.

In the early spring of 1893, a few weeks after Grover Cleveland started his second term in the White House, a motorcar moved through a Detroit street with Henry Ford on its single seat. He had built the automobile in the previous autumn, but months of testing were needed to make it run satisfactorily. It looked like an old-fashioned buggy. In his autobiography, *My Life and Work,* the inventor has described the car as follows:

There were two cylinders with a two-and-a-half-inch bore and a six-inch stroke set side by side and over the rear axle. I made them out of the exhaust pipe of a steam engine that I had bought. They developed about four horsepower. The power was transmitted from the motor to the countershaft by a belt and from the countershaft to the rear wheel by a chain. The car would hold two people, the seat being suspended on posts and the body on elliptical springs. There were two speeds—one of ten and the other of twenty miles an hour—obtained by shifting the belt, which was done by a clutch lever in front of the driving seat. Thrown forward, the lever put in the high speed; thrown back, the low speed; with the lever upright the engine could run free. To start the car it was necessary to turn the motor over by hand with the clutch free. To stop the car one simply released the clutch and applied the foot brake. There was no reverse, and speeds other than those of the belt were obtained by the throttle. I bought the ironwork for the frame of the carriage and also the seat and the springs. The wheels were twenty-eight-inch wire bicycle wheels with rubber tires. The balance wheel I had cast from a pattern that I made, and all of the more delicate mechanism I made myself. One of the features that I discovered necessary was a compensating gear that permitted the same power to be applied to each of the rear wheels when turning corners. The machine altogether weighed about five hundred pounds. A tank under the seat held three gallons of gasoline which was fed to the motor through a small pipe and a mixing valve. The ignition was by electric spark. The original machine was air-cooled—or, to be more accurate, the motor simply was not cooled at all. I found that on a run of an hour or more the motor heated up, and so I very shortly put a water jacket around the cylinders and piped it to a tank in the rear of the car over the cylinders.

An April rain had soothed Ford's neighbors to sleep when he bounced out of his yard on the eventful night in 1893, but such were the noises of his strange vehicle that the inhabitants were aroused forthwith. Faces appeared at all the windows roundabout. Mrs. Ford stood on the front steps, watching her husband as he vanished jolting and clattering into the farther reaches of Bagley Avenue.

For a long time the gasoline buggy was the only

FORD'S FIRST CAR—THE GASOLINE BUGGY
He finished building it in 1893, and for months it was one of the sights of Detroit.

automobile in Detroit. The police and the owners of frightened horses viewed it with suspicion. Wherever it appeared, traffic was blocked and curious pedestrians gathered to ask questions. The owner was obliged to tether the car to a lamp-post if he left it unattended, for somebody was always ready to take a chance at running it. At last he had to get a special permit from the mayor, thus acquiring, as he has related, "the distinction of being the only licensed chauffeur in America."

For the first performances of his automobile Henry

Ford happened to choose an eventful year. History, both scientific and political, was busy in the making through 1893. Edison invented his motion-picture machine. A peculiarly fitting coincidence of the year was the establishment of the Federal Office of Road Inquiry by Congressional order. Few if any of the Solons in Washington knew Henry Ford. None of them, in all probability, believed in horseless vehicles, nor indeed were the lawmakers of the nation or the states destined to show any faith in useful motor transport during that decade. The Federal Office of Road Inquiry and the new State Highway departments were due to the bicycle craze rather than the coming of motors. However, the

Three decades afterward—the same gasoline buggy.

movement for good roads began to find support at just the right time to aid in developing the motorcar. Toward the end of the year there was another spurt of concrete paving in Bellefontaine, the Ohio town which was for a long time the only community interested in the sort of road surface the whole country would eventually demand.

The year's record of notable events included the deaths of ex-President Rutherford B. Hayes, James G. Blaine, and Edwin Booth. Mayor Carter Harrison, Sr., of Chicago was assassinated. Two kings who now occupy their thrones were born, Carol of Rumania and Prajadhipok of Siam, and the motion-picture star, Mary Pickford. The World's Fair was opened in Chicago that year.

With omens of progress on all sides, Ford probably regarded the depression of '93, if he thought about it at all, as a passing phase which would be superseded by better and better times. In the miracle story of the Ford car optimism has been the keynote, from the gasoline buggy to the V-8. No panic could be so fearsome, no depression so disastrous, no war so terrible, that the Ford forecast failed to register a tide of rising prosperity. And behind the optimism was a continuing faith that the power of machinery and engineering must relieve mankind of drudgery and afford time for the enjoyment of life. While Henry Ford had not formulated in the two-cylinder epoch all his economic theories of later years, he was committed from boyhood to a supreme belief in the adequacy of science for maintaining the world's progress. The only delay in moving forward, as he demonstrated in his early experiments, was the caution which must temper a true scientist's enthusiasm. With such caution, but with a background of complete confidence, he proceeded to build engine after engine, car after car; eagerly though he sought to improve his product, he threw away no old ideas until study and tests proved the value of the new. His gasoline buggy of 1893 was as carefully planned and built, in view of the experience then available, as the more elaborate automobiles of later decades.

He ran this first car a thousand miles, sold it for two hundred dollars, because he needed the money, and after a few years bought it back to keep as a curio.

II
THE BEGINNING OF AN INDUSTRY

NEARLY THREE YEARS went by before Ford started to build his second car. The old gasoline buggy served his purposes for personal transportation, and he took his wife or a friend on a ride every now and then, until the novelty wore off. In his laboratory he spent all the time he could get, after finishing the day's shift on his job with the electric light company, which promoted him steadily until he was chief engineer at $125 a month.

The first automobile was only a milestone on the way toward the goal of quantity production. Ford was in no hurry. A lot of study, innumerable experiments, observation of the world's advances in science, were requisites for the inventor who could succeed in creating a car worth producing in quantities and who knew how to choose the right time for launching the business of motor manufacturing.

It would seem, from the vantage of the present, that no seer was needed to realize the deficiencies of transport in the early 'nineties. Isolation was the fate of all who dwelt outside of large cities. To visit a neighbor ten miles distant meant a day's travel, over roads often hub deep in mud, or with such ruts that locomotion in horse-drawn vehicles was as dangerous as it was slow. Towns and villages off the railway lines were hardly less desolate than the farms. Although electricity was coming into its own for rail travel in the cities, and a few towns were beginning to boast jerky trolley cars along their main streets, no interurban network was yet dreamed of.

In Europe the motor idea had progressed far enough in 1894 for a road race from Paris to Rouen. The win-

BEFORE MEN BELIEVED IN MOTORS
A Michigan farmhouse, facing an ancient country road and a primitive railway line.

ning car, which averaged twelve miles an hour, was regarded solely as a racing machine. None but a bold pilot would have dared to ride behind its roaring, sputtering engine.

As the financial depression crept on its course, causing widespread distress but apparently interfering not at all with the general trend of human affairs, science scored its points before the year ended. Lake perfected his invention of the even-keel submarine. A second city in America, Watertown, N. Y., laid down a section of concrete pavement.

The hard times brought continuous labor troubles. After the courts had enjoined Chicago's strikers, President Cleveland sent federal troops to the city to enforce order. This climax of walkouts by mine, factory, and railroad workers had been preceded by a countrywide uneasiness when "General" Jacob S. Coxey led an army

Detroit in 1890, before the skyscraper era.

of 20,000 unemployed from the Middle West to the National Capital. The Wilson tariff bill was passed, with the Democrats explaining that it would save the country, and Republicans predicting ruin: at least in that regard 1894 was like many other years.

On the other side of the earth began the Chinese-Japanese War, causing the same cry of "Yellow Peril" that has since echoed from each crisis in the Orient; the conflict was to end with Japan's taking the Liaotung Peninsula, Formosa, and the Pescadores, whereupon, though there were no long-distance airplanes in those days, prophets of disaster foretold the onrush of the yellow races across the western hemisphere. In Europe time marched on with the accession of Nicholas II as Czar of Russia. Edward Albert, Prince of Wales, was born in England. Boris, future King of Bulgaria, preceded him to this vale of troubles by a few months. The assassinated President of France, Sadi-Carnot, was succeeded by Casimir-Perier, and in the last days of the year Captain Dreyfus was publicly degraded as a traitor and sent to spend nearly twelve years on Devil's Island before his vindication brought him back to Paris.

The Ford experiment shop was not idle, though its owner was only testing and planning. He had already come to the conclusion which he phrased long afterward: "Rushing into manufacturing without being certain of the product is the unrecognized cause of many business failures."

Among the events of the year 1895, he doubtless regarded as most important the fact that California and Connecticut joined the states founding departments to encourage road improvements. He must have noted the death of Thomas Huxley in England. Incidents that would not have concerned him, if he had heard about them, were the election of Félix Faure to the Presidency of the French Republic, and the graduation of a young man named Herbert Hoover at Leland Stanford University. A new revolution in Cuba, lasting until its leader Antonio Maceo was killed in action the following year, was too remote from the Detroit workshop to merit much thought. More interesting were Preece's discovery of low-frequency wireless telegraphy in 1895, and Marconi's discovery of the high-frequency waves in

1896. Nearer home, though of small import to the scientist, was the seething national campaign, in which the free-silver issue, vainly championed by William J. Bryan, monopolized the political stage for two years before William McKinley's election to the Presidency in the fall of 1896.

Ford's second car, built that year, was lighter than the first but had the same belt drive, which he later supplanted with gears when he found that belts did not work well in hot weather. Meanwhile he had taken a trip to New York in 1895 to look at a Benz car, on exhibition in Macy's store. He found in it nothing to envy or imitate. The German invention was too heavy. Unlike the pioneer manufacturers abroad, Ford considered lightness a prime necessity in an automobile. For that reason he had become convinced that no steam engine could be made to propel a practical vehicle over the roads, and subsequent investigations of electric storage batteries ruled them out on the same ground. He continued his experiments with internal-combustion engines despite ridicule from practically everybody with whom he discussed the subject.

His introduction to Thomas A. Edison, who afterward became his intimate friend, was a memorable incident, for the master of electricity gave him encouragement which he had been unable to get from anybody else. Chosen as one of four men from the Detroit company to attend the annual convention of the Association of Edison Illuminating Companies at Manhattan Beach, N. Y., in 1896, he met Edison on the porch of the Oriental Hotel. Edison, who was forty-nine years old, found that Ford, who was nearing his thirty-third birthday, hailed from Detroit, so he kept him chatting about the country they both knew and the Grand Trunk Railroad. At the afternoon session and again at dinner the electric carriage was the main topic. Charles L. Edgar, president of the Boston company, sat at Edison's right, and Samuel Insull at his left. The head of the Detroit company, Alex Dow, pointed at Ford and remarked:

"There's a young fellow who has made a gas car."

Somebody asked how the vehicle worked, and Ford described it. Edgar traded seats with him, so that Edison could hear what was said. He plied the Detroiter with questions, and Ford made sketches showing all the details of the gasoline car, including the contact arrangement for exploding the gas in the cylinder and the insulating plug with make-and-break mechanism, prototype of the spark plug of today. Edison, when the catechism ended, brought his fist down on the table with a bang.

"Young man, that's the thing," he said. "You have it. Keep at it. Electric cars must keep near to power stations. The storage battery is too heavy. Steam cars won't do, either, for they require a boiler and a fire. Your car is self-contained—carries its own power plant —no fire, no boiler, no smoke, and no steam. You have the thing. Keep at it."

"That bang on the table," wrote Ford later, "was worth worlds to me. No man up to then had given me any encouragement. I had hoped that I was headed right, sometimes I knew that I was, sometimes I only wondered if I was, but here all at once and out of a clear sky the greatest inventive genius in the world had given me a complete approval. The man who knew most about electricity in the world had said that for the purpose my gas motor was better than any electric motor could be."

Even after Ford had built two cars, the scoffers of his home city were not impressed. The Edison Illuminating Company of Detroit offered to make him its general superintendent on condition that he would stop fooling with his gas engine and devote his time to useful work. That put squarely up to him the decision of his future course. He resigned his job in 1899 and went into the automobile business.

Meanwhile, with a mine strike and the passage of the Dingley Tariff Law as preliminary episodes, good times began to replace depression in 1897, and within the year the Klondike gold rush started, the Turkish-Greek War was fought, the union of five counties into the City of Greater New York was effected, and Salomon August Andrée set out from Sweden with two companions to drift his balloon over the North Pole, an exploit which remained a mystery of the Arctic until three bodies and the balloon's wreckage were found thirty-three years later. Our war with Spain was the big news of 1898, beginning with the breach of diplomatic relations in April, after public prejudice had been aroused to incredible excess by an explosion that wrecked the battleship *Maine* in Havana harbor on February 15th. The Spaniards' Pacific fleet was destroyed by Admiral George Dewey's fighting ships on May 1st, and Spain's débâcle came when their Atlantic fleet under Cervera was annihilated off Santiago on July 3d, at the same time that the near-by land battles at San Juan Hill and

El Caney were making a hero and future President out of Lieutenant-Colonel Theodore Roosevelt of the Rough Riders.

On the day after the Santiago victory, July 4th, the North Atlantic Ocean witnessed a tragedy that focussed world-wide attention on the backwardness of science in providing safeguards against marine casualties. A French steamship of the first class, the *Bourgogne,* ran into the British sailing ship *Cromartyshire.* Five hundred and sixty lives were lost. Whatever so-called modern improvements the *Bourgogne* possessed were of no avail amid the waves and fog. The story of fragile bulkheads, inadequate lifeboats, and undisciplined crews stayed in the memory of the public, and resulted in a marked increase in the efforts of shipowners to protect their passengers—although it remained for a greater disaster nearly two decades afterward to point the way toward a real measure of safety at sea. There had been, of course, thousands of ghastly accidents through the ages in which human knowledge was inadequate to cope with the elements. Back in 1893 the liner *Naronic* started from Liverpool on her maiden voyage and disappeared without a trace; in 1894 the steamship *Norge* sank with 600 souls aboard; in every season ships large and small went to the bottom, with no wireless to call for help or to announce their helplessness. The sinking of the *Bourgogne* involved no greater loss of life than many another wreck, but the news of it horrified a generation which was beginning to believe its civilization an equal antagonist of Nature's forces.

If there was one invention in which the public of that period did not believe, however, it was the "horseless vehicle." There was no demand for practical automobiles when Henry Ford determined to manufacture them; no faith in their future, no financial backing for their few advocates.

As an excuse for the public's lack of vision, it may be recalled that in those stirring years men were confronted with many happenings they could understand better than the gasoline engine. The South African War was bleeding Britain and killing off the Boers. We had a civil war of our own in the Philippines, where Aguinaldo would not stop rebelling against the new order. The Russian Czar called together a Universal Peace Conference, the first of its kind, at The Hague. The game of golf was gaining a foothold in this country, though its devotees met with almost as much ridicule as did the motorcar pioneers. Diesel invented his oil motor in 1900, and the world's savants lamented the passing of Friedrich W. Nietzsche, of whom it has been said that no other man had more influence on modern thought. In the same year Galveston was devastated by a tidal flood; the Boxer uprising upset old China and caused armies to be rushed thither by the Western nations; William McKinley was reëlected President, an assassin struck down King Humbert of Italy, and the Paris Exposition was opened.

The next year, 1901, saw the end of Queen Victoria's reign and Edward VII on the British throne. Ex-President Benjamin Harrison died, and the present Emperor Hirohito of Japan was born. Wall Street had a short panic when somebody cornered Northern Pacific stock. Theodore Roosevelt became President after McKinley was slain by an assassin at the Buffalo Exposition. As the year came to a close, Marconi signaled the letter S across the ocean from England to Newfoundland, a preliminary to sending the first radio message oversea a few months later.

With the new century under full steam ahead, seven of the states had got their highway departments going. Bicyclists by tens of thousands were on the roads, and a few racing motorcars. Henry Ford has said in his autobiography:

> When it was found that an automobile really could go and several makers started to put out cars, the immediate query was as to which would go fastest. It was a curious but natural development—that racing idea. I never thought anything of racing, but the public refused to consider the automobile in any light other than as a fast toy. Therefore later we had to race. The industry was held back by this initial racing slant, for the attention of the makers was diverted to making fast rather than good cars. It was a business for speculators.

As soon as he left the electric company, he gathered a group of men who were speculators enough to form the Detroit Automobile Company, in which he held a small part of the stock. He was the manager and chief engineer; in fact, he ran the concern, while the others waited for their profits. Few cars were sold, hardly any money was made, and just before the third birthday of the experiment Ford decided to resign and to be his own boss for the rest of his life. He rented a one-story brick shed and went on with his experiments in 1902, trying out engines and building improved models on the principle of his first car.

It was in this period that he gave serious thought to the invention of tractors for the farmers, although fifteen years were to elapse before he put them on the market. In fact, the tractor idea had been in the back of his head since he became interested, as a young boy, in a clumsy road engine propelled by steam and used for operating sawmills and threshing machines. From the time he started making automobiles there was not a year in which he did not make experiments looking toward the tractor, but, as he has since remarked, "the public was more interested in being carried than in being pulled; the horseless carriage made a greater appeal to the imagination. And so it was that I practically dropped work upon a tractor until the automobile was in production. With the automobile on the farms, the tractor became a necessity. For then the farmers had been introduced to power." In after years, when he saw practical results multiply from his interest in agricultural machinery, he was to issue an order giving leaves of absence to those among his army of employees who wished to work their farms.

While he was busy on a four-cylinder motor in his one-room shop in 1902, the racing mania grew. The track champion, Alexander Winton of Cleveland, let it be known that he was ready to meet all comers. Ford designed a compact two-cylinder engine, fitted it on a skeleton chassis, made a few trial runs that proved the car could make speed, and arranged a meeting with Winton. They raced on the Grosse Point track, Detroit. Ford won. It was his first race, and he got a vast deal of advertising "of the only kind that people cared to read."

Two big racing cars were then produced in the little shop, with the assistance of Tom Cooper. They named one the 999 and the other the *Arrow*. The engines were nearly alike, and developed eighty horsepower. The

ONE OF FORD'S RACING CARS
In his early years as a manufacturer, he attracted the public's attention by speed machines.

cylinders roared with a deafening noise, and the inventor says he has never found words adequate for describing the sensation of himself and Cooper when they made their trials.

They decided to enter 999 in a race in 1903, but neither of them was willing to be the pilot. Cooper said he knew a bicycle rider who wasn't afraid. So they wired to Barney Oldfield, who came from Salt Lake City, looked over the motorcar, and said he would try anything once. He learned to drive in a week. While the preparations were being carried on with great secrecy, he managed to master the two-handed tiller with which the steering was done by sheer strength. The race was a three-mile affair on a track not properly banked, but Oldfield took the curves at full speed. At the end he won by half a mile in front of the second car.

One week after the race the Ford Motor Company was formed, with Henry Ford as vice president, designer, master mechanic, superintendent, general manager, and holder of 25½ per cent of the $100,000 of capital stock, of which $28,000 was in cash. That was the only money the company ever received for the capital fund except from operations. A few years later the inventor acquired a 51 per cent control of the company. Then he bought up to 58½ per cent. It was not until 1919 that his son Edsel purchased all the remainder of the stock at $12,500 a share.

The sport of motor racing, into which Ford had embarked merely to let people know he could make cars, had served its purpose so far as he was concerned. For the public it vied with the news of world affairs through the two years the inventor had been planning his new start in business.

There were many excitements besides sports in the news of 1902 and 1903, however. In the first year Stribblefield invented the radio sending apparatus, Poulsen and Tessenden talked over their wireless telephone, Korn sent a photograph over the wires, and the first radio message came across the Atlantic Ocean. Government activities were keyed to the high pitch that distinguished "T. R.'s" terms in the White House; the Panama Canal purchase was authorized, civil government established in the Philippine Islands, the Northern Securities' Anti-Trust decision announced, the Cuban Republic inaugurated, the anthracite strike settled by Presidential intervention, Alfonso XIII enthroned in Spain at the age of eighteen after a long regency, the South African War ended, and 30,000 lives snuffed out on the island of Martinique by the eruption of the Mt. Pelée volcano. Another event of 1902, to be chronicled twenty-five years afterward in the halls of fame, was the birth of Charles A. Lindbergh, Jr.

While it would be impossible to find in the records of 1903 a happening that exerted more influence on the generation than the launching of the Ford industry, many other things caused a larger commotion at the time. The Department of Commerce and Labor was organized, the Pacific cable completed, the Alaska boundary dispute settled, and the Canal Treaty with Panama ratified. The Panamanian Republic's recognition by this country aroused a controversy which is argued to this day, with proponents equally violent for and against "T. R.'s" connection with the Canal purchase and the ensuing revolution. The Iroquois Theatre fire in Chicago caused the loss of 602 lives. Overseas, the happenings of the year included the Kisheneff massacre and the election of Pope Pius X to succeed Leo XIII.

The Wright brothers' achievement in the final month of 1903 will figure in history as one of the scientific triumphs of all time. There is a striking similarity between their early struggles and the beginnings of Henry Ford. The world scoffed while Orville and Wilbur Wright quietly developed a heavier-than-air flying machine in Dayton, just as it ridiculed Ford's gasoline buggy. Nor did skepticism vanish when they took their frail craft to Kitty Hawk, N. C., and over the sandy beach realized a dream which had held the fancy of inventors for centuries, a sustained flight in an airplane carrying its own motive power. The flying machine, like the motorcar, was to be viewed as a racing toy for many a year.

Meanwhile the safety bicycle, succeeding the old high-wheel affair, had become recognized as a practical and pleasant means of travel. More than three hundred factories were making bicycles in the United States. There were clubs of cyclists all over the world. The paraphernalia of "tripping," as the English would say, had to be compressed into tiny spaces on the "bike," but the handy kits of the early 'nineties were capacious enough to satisfy hordes of men and women. Vacations awheel were the rage. The hotels of the country and the roadside restaurants flourished. Quick journeys between towns a score or more miles apart were possible for the first time, for those who could not afford railway fares. The world's taste for travel had grown almost overnight—an augury of the motorcar's triumph, though few besides Henry Ford sensed it.

Of the venturesome associates whom he persuaded to join him in founding the Ford Motor Company, the first was a coal man, Malcolmson. Next came Couzens, a clerk in Malcolmson's office, now a United States

Senator; Gray, a manufacturing confectioner and friend of Malcolmson; the two Dodges, owners of a Detroit machine shop that agreed to make 650 motors for the new concern; Woodall, who was Malcolmson's bookkeeper; Fry, a bookkeeper; Bennett, an employee of a company making toy guns; Strelow, a carpenter who really believed in motorcars, and two lawyers, Rackham and Anderson. No bankers participated. The investors were the objects of much ridicule among their acquaintances. Except for Strelow, who sold his fifty shares before the company got well started and lost the proceeds in a mining venture, they had the last laugh. Before many years passed their profits would have made Aladdin envious.

The company rented a carpenter shop in Mack Avenue, Detroit, where its equipment consisted of a few models of engines and cars and a little machinery. The plan was to buy from different manufacturers the engines, bodies, wheels, tires, and parts, and assemble the cars according to designs worked out by Ford. There was not enough cash on hand or in sight to start much of a manufacturing business. If the prices were right, it made no difference to Ford whether he constructed or purchased, though, as it turned out in the ensuing years, the company gradually took on all the phases of the industry in order to produce at the lowest cost and to insure the uniform quality of materials.

One of the most impressive aspects of the Ford development, from the very start, was the attitude of the inventor as distinguished from that of others who invested in motorcar enterprises. Most of them had no vision beyond the immediate profits from cars built for racing or for the diversion of the well-to-do; the automobile was to be like an expensive bicycle, but with more speed and more space for baggage; the objective of the makers generally was to get as much money as the traffic would bear, without regard to durability which would cause the customer to buy other cars in the future. Ford, on the other hand, foresaw a market for 95 per cent of the population, with prices low and quality lasting. His basic idea of service, as contrasted to quick returns, was formulated before his manufacturing amounted to anything.

Business as it was run in those days—and to a decreasing extent in later years—meant grabbing all the cash one could squeeze out of a customer, who thereafter could go to the devil. Whether a motorcar would stand up, how much gasoline it needed, whether the parts could be replaced, were problems outside the concern of the manufacturer. It was in this atmosphere that Ford, practically alone, determined to build up an honest business, in which service would be the keynote and profits the result only of value received. That has been the motive behind the Ford car. To what extent it has influenced other lines of business, educating the buying public to protect itself from exploitation, is a question which can be answered by any thoughtful observer of industrial progress in the last four decades.

III
PERFORMANCE AND PROFITS

THE BUSINESS OF THE COMPANY prospered as if by magic. While Ford expected profits, growing with the years, performance and permanence were the main aims in his policy. Other stockholders, under the spell of the current delusion that fickleness in public taste required frequent changes of design for motorcars, were able to make their influence felt in the few years when he lacked a controlling interest in the organization; but his domination of the technical side was such that he sacrificed his opinions only in superficial matters. Although he made many models and still entered cars in speed tests, he built each new automobile strong enough to last and as far as possible provided interchangeable parts, in order to keep the car in service as long as the buyer desired to use it, even long after other cars of the same vintage were ready for scrapping.

In the first year of the Ford Motor Company, Model A made its appearance. It was priced at $850, but the lamps, horn, and windshield were extras. In form it was a sort of runabout. A tonneau could be lifted on to make it a touring car, and this elaborated shape sold for $950. The two cylinders developed 8 horsepower, the wheelbase was 72 inches, and the fuel capacity 5 gallons. Sales for the year numbered 1,708 cars.

The inventor has traced the history of these Model

A's. One of them, No. 420, typifies their ability to stand the test of time and hard usage. Colonel D. C. Collier of California, the purchaser, used it two years before getting another Ford. It changed hands several times and in 1907 was bought by a man living in the mountains, where he ran the car over the roughest of roads. He too sold his old Ford and got a new one. By 1915 this Model A was owned by one Cantello, who took out the motor and connected it with a water pump, while the chassis was put into service as a buggy, drawn by a burro.

"The moral, of course, is that you can dissect a Ford, but you cannot kill it," remarks the inventor in his autobiography.

Primitive as the early cars seem to us today, the creations of the Ford Motor Company in its first years caused a vast boom in motoring. Though there had been an increase of passable rural roads for the bicyclists' benefit, the hard surfacing of highways was in its infancy. Dust clouds assailed the tourist. The automobile owner and his wife and children wore linen dusters, and the driver required goggles to keep his eyesight equal to the strain of going twenty miles an hour. Acetylene lamps lighted the way at night. The car contained room for more baggage than a bicycle, but the space was occupied largely by tools, extra parts, and materials for patching tires. Women motorists wore veils, and some members of the traveling family kept a diary of the exciting journeys into neighboring counties, recording the exact minutes of departure and arrival, the speed maintained, and the adventures along the road. And there were adventures aplenty. Ripping off a disabled tire with a chisel was one frequent experience. Crawling underneath the engine to make repairs was another. But automobiling was worth all the trouble it involved.

Until the Ford idea permeated the country, motor vehicles had been for the rich. It was estimated that in 1903 Americans spent $1,000,000 for foreign cars, and the sum trebled in two years. An embryo motor show in New York, about the time the Ford Company was formed, included four toy cars costing as little as $500. A real motor vehicle in those days brought from $1,000 to $8,000; those below $2,000 were rickety affairs, and the more expensive ones were not much hardier.

Ford never made an appeal to buyers who were merely on pleasure bent. While the owners of Ford cars probably got as much fun out of their travels as the idlest plutocrats, the argument which attracted them was the new selling appeal of service. The first advertisement of the company read:

> Our purpose is to construct and market an automobile specially designed for everyday wear and tear—business, professional, and family use; an automobile which will attain to a sufficient speed to satisfy the average person without acquiring any of those break-neck velocities which are so universally condemned; a machine which will be admired by man, woman, and child alike for its compactness, its simplicity, its safety, its all-around convenience, and—last but not least—its exceedingly reasonable price, which places it within the reach of many thousands who could not think of paying the comparatively fabulous prices asked for most machines.

The Ford salesmen were taught to emphasize the good materials used in making the cars, the simplicity of operation, the engine, the ignition, the automatic oiling, the planetary transmission, and the workmanship.

One advertisement included the following description of the new car:

We often hear quoted the old proverb, "Time is Money" —and yet how few business and professional men act as if they really believed its truth.

Men who are constantly complaining of shortage of time and lamenting the fewness of days in the week—men to whom every five minutes wasted means a dollar thrown away—men to whom five minutes' delay sometimes means the loss of many dollars—will yet depend on the haphazard, uncomfortable, and limited means of transportation afforded by street cars, etc., when the investment of an exceedingly moderate sum in the purchase of a perfected, efficient, high-grade automobile would cut out anxiety and unpunctuality and provide a luxurious means of travel ever at your beck and call.

Always ready, always sure.

Built to save you time and consequent money.

Built to take you anywhere you want to go and bring you back again on time.

Built to add to your reputation for punctuality; to keep your customers good-humored and in a buying mood.

Built for business or pleasure—just as you say.

Built also for the good of your health—to carry you "jarlessly" over any kind of half-decent roads, to refresh your brain with the luxury of much "outdoorness" and your lungs with the "tonic of tonics"—the right kind of atmosphere.

It is your say, too, when it comes to speed. You can—if you choose—loiter lingeringly through shady avenues or you can press down on the foot-lever until all the scenery looks alike to you and you have to keep your eyes skinned to count the milestones as they pass.

Before the company was making enough money to carry on scientific investigations as to the finest and lightest materials, but was getting the best the market afforded, the reputation of the efficient low-priced car increased rapidly. The frontiers of states and counties were swept away. The touring habit spread over the land. It has been often said that Ford and his associates taught Americans to know America. That truism need not be confined to America. Soon the influence of their pioneering extended over the world.

In the second year the company offered three models. They were lettered B, C, and F: a four-cylinder touring car, for $2,000; a slightly improved Model A, at a price $50 above its prototype, and a touring car for $1,000. The result of scattered energies and higher prices was a decrease in sales from 1,706 to 1,695 cars. This furnished a lesson from which the inventor eventually profited.

If there had been statistics showing popular interest in news events, the progress of the Ford idea would have made a big showing in the figures. Yet the news of the period, in which "T. R.'s" glamorous personality dominated the political field, was by no means confined to science or invention. In the year 1904 Russia and Japan went to war, the St. Louis exposition opened, the business section of Baltimore was devastated by fire, and the first New York subway was completed. A train on the Philadelphia and Reading Railroad made a speed record of 115.20 miles an hour for a distance of 4.8 miles. Franklin D. Roosevelt finished his course at Harvard. One of the most gruesome disasters of our times, the burning of the steamboat *General Slocum* on the East River at New York, cost the lives of 1,021 holiday picnickers, mostly children.

The happening of most influence on Henry Ford's plans was the organization of the United States Office of Public Roads, which, succeeding the old Office of Road Inquiry, ordered a census of the nation's highways. This showed 2,151,590 miles of rural roads, of which 153,662 miles were surfaced with materials then regarded as satisfactory. Coincidental with Models B, C, and F, the country was showing real interest in good roads, though modern concrete was yet a substance with which only small experiments had been made; the only pavings of that material were laid in four or five scattered towns. The total expenditures of the year 1904 on country highways was $79,595,418, hardly one twentieth of the annual outlay a quarter of a century later.

Model B was the first four-cylinder car for general road use. Deciding that racing victories were still the best advertising, Ford remade his old *Arrow,* and a week before the New York Automobile Show he drove it a mile straightaway on the ice, in 39 2/5 seconds. When he got under way, he discovered that the frozen course was seamed with fissures, each of which sent the car leaping into the air. Every time it leaped, he wondered if he would come down right side up. Between leaps he skidded this way and that. Finally the mile was covered, in record time that made news the world over. Model B became famous. Yet, as Ford has since pointed out, no amount of stunt racing or advertising could overcome price advances. Gradually he was being educated in the business of making the motorcar a more paying product by lowering its cost.

The jokesters of the press, meanwhile, were not yet silenced, and even in serious editorials the automobile continued to be an object of attack. The "devil wagon," as it was called by the scoffers, was depicted as a symbol of snobbery. Not only were the poor farmer's cows and chickens its victims, but gloomy prophets predicted great loss of human life unless the racers were curbed. At best they described the nuisance of gasoline fumes and hideous noises as the average man's penalty for allowing the rich to possess such toys. That this sort of gibing soon ceased was due to Ford's rapid success in turning the critics into enthusiastic owners and drivers.

In 1905 and 1906 he made only two models, a four-cylinder car at $2,000 and another touring car at $1,000. Again there was a drop in sales, to 1,599. It was now that Ford took matters into his own hands, acquiring control of the company's stock and outvoting his partners for the first time. The wooden carpenter shop was superseded by a three-story plant, giving him real manufacturing facilities. In 1906-07 touring cars were abandoned and three runabouts built. They differed little from the previous models, though they looked different. The cheapest was sold for $600, the most expensive for $750. Sales jumped to 8,423. Turning back to the touring shape in the next year, the inventor designed a fast six-cylinder fifty-horse-power car, but continued to produce the low-priced models. Sales dropped. Ford was convinced that the decrease was due to the more expensive model as well as to the business panic of 1907. He decided not to experiment with high-priced cars again. Nor did he enter the six-cylinder field again.

The try-outs of the early years had run the gamut of Ford's experience and imagination. The cars he designed had ranged in horsepower from eight to forty; they had been built with two, four, and six cylinders, and minor changes in construction had been innumerable. "The only thing in the world that never changes is change itself," said the manufacturer, paraphrasing an old epigram. By 1908 he had sold eight models and constructed eleven others which were not put on the market.

Meanwhile, the world moved forward—more rapidly than was its wont before men grew motor-wise. Remote regions joined in the demand for good roads. The Japanese humiliated Russia in 1905, ending the war with the capture of Port Arthur; Norway broke her union with Sweden; an investigation of the insurance companies brought into public notice a rising New York lawyer, Charles E. Hughes, now Chief Justice of the United States Supreme Court; Joseph Jefferson and Sir Henry Irving died; Greta Garbo was born. In the next year, 1906, earthquake and fire almost destroyed San Francisco, after quakes had killed thousands in Japan's outlying island of Formosa; the United States occupied Cuba for a second time; Hendrik Ibsen died, and the year's births included Emperor Henry Pu Yi of

China and Manchukuo, and Joan Crawford of movie-
dom. In 1907 the popularity of concrete city paving
made its first real stride, on three streets in Chicago, one
in New Haven and one in Salt Lake City; Lee de Forest
invented the vacuum radio tube; the United States

Model K—the only six-cylinder Ford car.

fleet was ordered by "T. R." to make a voyage around
the world; Oklahoma became a state; the Federal Pure
Food Law went into effect; Gustav V became King of
Sweden; the American stage lost its foremost actor,
Richard Mansfield.

Henry Ford, having confirmed his belief that the
increase of aggregate profits was in direct proportion
to the smallness of the profit on each car, was getting
ready for mass production.

A sales organization, carefully expanded each year,
was working full speed. At first it had been hard to

find good salesmen. The men who could sell were wary about entering what was considered an unstable business. Ford gradually perfected his selling force by selecting able men and offering them larger salaries than they could earn in business for themselves. As he recalled later:

> In the beginning we had not paid much in the way of salaries. We were feeling our way, but when we knew what our way was, we adopted the policy of paying the very highest reward for service and then insisting upon getting the highest service.

Besides the sales agents' energy and initiative, a clean and suitable place of business was demanded. A sufficient supply of parts had to be on hand to keep in active service all Ford cars in the representative's territory, and he must have an adequate repair shop, with mechanics thoroughly familiar with the construction and operation of the cars. Every agent undertook to do proper bookkeeping and to maintain a follow-up sales system and records of his customers present or prospective; to see that no dirty windows or floors marred his showroom, to display a suitable sign outside, and to cultivate a reputation for square dealing.

While Ford was working against odds both in the manufacturing and sales ends, the famous Selden patent suit was a sore trial, though eventually it resulted in some of the best advertising he ever had. The suit was an attempt to force him into line with an association of automobile manufacturers operating under the belief that there was only a limited market for motorcars and that a monopoly of the market was necessary. George B. Selden himself had little to do with the action.

Back in 1879, Selden, who was a patent attorney, filed an application for a patent with the stated object of producing "a safe, simple, and cheap road locomotive, light in weight, easy to control, possessed of sufficient power to overcome ordinary inclination." The patent was granted in 1895. In the interval Selden had done nothing to put his idea into practice, while several inventors had developed vehicles propelled by motors.

A group of manufacturers, acquiring a "license" to use the Selden patent, brought suit against the Ford Company as soon as it began to make a success of motorcar production. In 1909, after volumes had been filled with testimony, Judge Hough of the United States District Court rendered a decision in favor of the "licensed manufacturers," whose association at once advertised a warning to prospective Ford buyers. This they had also done at the beginning of the suit, in 1903.

Ford, who was confident the Hough decision would not stand, proceeded to reassure his customers. They were being told, he learned, that every owner of a Ford car would be prosecuted if the suit was finally won by the allied manufacturers, and even that they might be sent to jail! An advertisement to counteract this propaganda was published promptly. It ended as follows:

> In conclusion we beg to state if there are any prospective automobile buyers who are at all intimidated by the claims made by our adversaries that we will give them, in addition

to the protection of the Ford Motor Company with its some $6,000,000.00 of assets, an individual bond backed by a Company of more than $6,000,000.00 more of assets, so that each and every individual owner of a Ford car will be protected until at least $12,000,000.00 of assets have been wiped out by those who desire to control and monopolize this wonderful industry.

The bond is yours for the asking, so do not allow yourself to be sold inferior cars at extravagant prices because of any statement made by this "Divine" body.

N.B.—This fight is not being waged by the Ford Motor Company without the advice and counsel of the ablest patent attorneys of the East and West.

Only about fifty car buyers asked for the bond, although more than eighteen thousand cars were sold that year. The public's sympathy was on Ford's side. His company was being attacked by a combination with resources of seventy million dollars, whereas it had at the beginning not half that number of thousands.

In spite of the suit, which still was to drag on for a long time before the association lost out, the year 1908 found Ford with plenty of experience and enough money to go ahead with his ambitious plans.

He had toyed for years with the thought of a strong car so cheap that well-nigh everybody could afford to buy it. To concentrate on one model, the best he could devise, and with it to tap the vast market as yet untouched, now became his goal. His partners thought he had gone mad. His salesmen, though less vocal, had the same opinion. Nobody could understand why he was willing to abandon the enormous profits the com-

A small Ford village industry. Operated by water power.

A country flour mill turned into a Ford village industry. Operated by water power.

pany had been piling up: two million dollars in five years, an increase of ten thousand per cent for the original investors! Why not go ahead on the old line, they pleaded, erect a fine administration building and a big plant, and let the millions accumulate? But their laments had no effect on the man who was now the boss.

Three years previously, in 1905, a year before he acquired control of the company's stock and three years before he made his final plunge away from old methods, there had been a great motor race on Long Island for the Vanderbilt Cup. Among the spectators was Ford. He was looking at the wreckage of a French car when he made a discovery destined to influence his whole career. With the thought that the foreign engines had better parts than those of American make, he picked up a valve strip stem from the tangle of metal. What was the material that made this part so strong and yet so light? Nobody could tell him. Giving the stem to an assistant, he told him to find out all about it.

Discovering that it was made of a French steel containing vanadium, he made inquiries of all the steel makers in America, but was informed that not one could turn out vanadium steel. An expert was imported from England, and a small company in Ohio undertook to run a furnace with 3,000 degrees of heat requisite for manufacturing the material, provided Ford would guarantee it against loss. The first test was a failure, but finally he got his vanadium steel of 170,000 pounds tensile strength, an increase from the 60,000 to 70,000 pounds strength hitherto regarded as a maximum. Thereupon he had his models torn to pieces and tested every part to see what sort of steel was best for each—a hard steel, or a tough steel, or an elastic steel. Of the twenty types of steel selected, ten contained vanadium, which was used wherever strength and lightness were needed. Not all the ten had the same amount of vanadium. The composition varied according to whether the parts required spring or must stand hard wear.

The experiments with vanadium were epochal in automobile construction, for previously not more than four different grades of steel had been used in cars. Ford continued his tests in later years, always aiming at a further increase in strength and a decrease in weight. He often said of his proposed "universal car" that it must be strong, light, and foolproof, and a slogan he adopted was, "When one of my cars breaks down I know I am to blame."

The banner week of the Ford Motor Company in the five trial years was the second week of May, 1908. In the small factory 311 cars were finished in six days. On a single day in the following June 100 cars were assembled. Ford was set to build what he announced as the "universal car."

Mass production was not a new term in 1908. Years previously there had been machine-made steel parts, typewriters, bicycles, boots, cloth patterns, and what not. But to standardize the machine manufacture of a complex automobile, with its five thousand parts, was regarded as impossible. How could machines be devised to manufacture the multitude of variously shaped parts made of metals, leather, glass, and wood needed for even the smallest motorcar? Yet that was just what Ford determined to do.

His conception of the word "standardization," however, was based on the assumption that a vast majority of the buying public, say 95 per cent, would continue to purchase an article only when convinced that its quality was the best obtainable at the price quoted. He knew that too often manufacturers looked upon standardization as a system of making something to sell at a high price without regard to quality, with the result that their market became flooded with goods nobody would buy. It was his opinion then, and still is, that buying power always exists when the price is right. Merely to cut prices does not make an article worth buying. The customers must be "shown." Prove to them that a manufacturer habitually gives the best values, and they remain his patrons. The Ford car in all its phases has benefited from public confidence. Its standardization has involved constant reductions of price as frequently as economies at the factories made a lower price possible.

"The price has to be reduced," explains Ford, "because of the manufacturing economies that have come about, and not because the falling demand by the public indicates that it is not satisfied with the price. The public should always be wondering how it is possible to give so much for the money."

So he embarked upon the great adventure of the "universal car." He was going to his ruin, predicted his competitors—perhaps not without satisfaction. His stockholders figuratively tore their hair and tried in vain to stop him.

IV
THE "UNIVERSAL CAR," MODEL T

A MONTH BEFORE WILLIAM H. TAFT was elected President of the United States, in the autumn of 1908, Henry Ford offered for sale an automobile the like of which had not been seen, nor imagined except by its maker, since the motor industry came into being. Model T, the "universal car," defied the traditions of the other pioneers, violated their prejudices against simplicity and economy in automobiles, and started on its long career amid the gibes of the manufacturing world.

Simplicity was the chief trait of the new model. The engine, frame, and axles were easily accessible, and no mechanical genius was needed for mending or replacements. Most of the parts cost so little that buying new ones was more economical than repairing them. The important features had all been tested in one or another of the inventor's previous models. The price of the touring car was $850, and there were a town car for $1,000, a roadster for $825, a coupé for $950, and a landaulet for $950. Each variation was a simple Model T with no frills. In the first year 10,607 cars were sold, breaking all records in the industry.

In the next eighteen years this plain rival of the ornate vehicles hitherto characteristic of the automobile market was to revolutionize road transportation. The calamitous events of the period passed unheeded by

Model T. The Ford evolution, leaving all competitors behind, proceeded without a reverse through nearly two decades in which the world turned topsy-turvy. The Woodrow Wilson tide rose and fell. War wrecked Europe. Governments were overthrown, customs uprooted, beliefs of the older generation cast aside. The United States, dragged into the conflict, emerged in a condition of hysteria which was reflected in a revival of political conservatism, extreme changes in manners, and a nation-wide nervousness over the "Red menace" that Bolshevist influence was supposed to impose upon us. But there was no halt during those years in the advance of industry, in which Ford's mass production was the dominant force.

Contemporaneous developments in science and business included the radio and the airplane. The motion-picture craze, already well under way, reached a climax in a national censorship. Peace movements resulting from the long war occupied the attention of the thoughtful but had little effect on the multitude, intent upon resuming its interrupted routine. For the first time science and mechanics took precedence over the study of classics in our schools and colleges, indicating that the war had turned men's minds from the cultural to the practical.

A coincidence of 1908 was the fact that the first mile of rural concrete road was completed in Wayne County, Michigan, about the same time Ford announced his Model T in that county. Good roads and the motorcar were to grow in popularity thenceforth, each a complement to the other. The year was notable for the earthquake disaster in Sicily and Calabria, causing the loss of 76,000 lives and wrecking the city of Messina; the assassination of the Portuguese King, Carlos, and the death of ex-President Grover Cleveland.

The ways of the world had changed fast in the space of a lifetime. With America crisscrossed by railroads, cities in constant communication by telegraph and

The first Model T, 1908–1909.

telephone, every town "covered" by its newspaper belonging to one of the two great news associations, and the building of surfaced roads at last regarded as a necessity, the public was ready for whatever innovation would increase the compactness of the country. In the next five years Ford was to put half a million Model T's on the road and assemble them at the rate of 800 a day in his Highland Park plant near Detroit.

It was in 1909 that he formally announced his policy of uniformity, although no year passed without changes

in the details of Model T's construction, which remained its unadorned self in exterior appearance. Model
T was in constant evolution before "yearly models"
seized the industry.

A few more miles of concrete roads were built in
1909, a year of famous achievements. Peary reached the
North Pole in the spring. The Payne-Aldrich tariff bill
was enacted. Scott and Shackleton got started on their
Antarctic expeditions. Albert I became King of the
Belgians. Louis Blériot flew over the English Channel
in an airplane, from Calais to Dover. The first use of
the wireless telegraph to save lives at sea thrilled the
civilized world when the steamship *Republic* sank after
crashing into the *Florida* off Nantucket Island; only six
deaths resulted; answering the C Q D signal from
Jack Binns, the *Republic's* wireless operator, the *Baltic*
and other vessels raced to the scene of the wreck and
flashed the news over the Seven Seas. While the ensuing
year saw a feverish increase in automobile sales, news
from the nation's capital included the establishment of
the Commerce Court and the Postal Savings Banks, and
the accession of Edward D. White as Chief Justice
of the United States Supreme Court. In Europe the
kingdom of Portugal was replaced by a republic after
autocratic rule for 800 years, and Edward VII was
succeeded by George V as King of England. The year
1911, when the Ford Motor Company got its real start
in England by selling 14,000 cars after several seasons
of ineffectual efforts to gain a foothold, was marked by
the Supreme Court decisions dissolving the Standard
Oil and American Tobacco Companies. That was the
climax of the "trust-busting" era. Late in the year the

phenomenon of Woodrow Wilson, the New Dealer of his day, began to impress political wiseacres, though the rank and file did not yet foresee the upset which was impending in our national government. In China the Manchu Dynasty was overthrown and a republic proclaimed. The Italian-Turkish War began. C. P. Rogers made the first transcontinental air flight, in the actual flying time of 84 hours and 2 minutes. Amundsen discovered the South Pole a fortnight before the year ended, to be followed a month later by Scott, who lost his life on the return trip toward his base.

Besides witnessing the Bull Moose movement and the election of Wilson to the Presidency over Taft and Theodore Roosevelt, the year 1912 found the two new states of Arizona and New Mexico admitted to the Union. A Balkan war, forerunner of the World War, caused no alarm over here. State and local highway authorities generally became interested in concrete, which now surfaced a total of two hundred and fifty miles of rural roads. The beginning of the country's motor-bus network resulted from the revolution in Mexico, when an American miner, A. L. Hayes, fleeing across the border to California, decided to make a living by hauling passengers from San Diego to near-by towns; he rented a second-hand car, soon had a small fleet of them, and established the Pickwick Line, later absorbed by the Greyhound System.

On the night of April 14-15, 1912, occurred the most sensational marine disaster of modern times, the sinking of the *Titanic*. Heralded as the perfect steamship, with safety bulkheads and every other safeguard science could suggest to make her "unsinkable," the ocean giant carried more than 2,000 passengers, of whom 1,517 perished, including 103 women and 53 children. Speeding through waters dotted with icebergs, regardless of wireless warnings of the danger, the *Titanic* felt a dull thud that was hardly noticed at first by the joyous throng in the ballroom and the early sleepers in their staterooms. The orchestra played. Men and women sat undisturbed at the card tables. The last night of the voyage, with New York less than a day away, was a night of revelry for the cabin contingent. Only in the forward steerage, down by the water line, was there evidence of the fatal gash which a jagged knife of ice had cut in the vessel's side.

Slowly the water poured in, through bulkheads that could not be closed. An hour passed before even the ship's officers realized that the "unsinkable" *Titanic* was mortally wounded. The orchestra played on. Lifeboats, of which too few had been provided, were launched with half as many passengers as they should have held. Still nobody believed the vessel was sinking. "See you at breakfast," a man shouted from the promenade deck to a woman in one of the boats. After panic seized the steerage, laughter still echoed through the cabin saloons. It was long past midnight when the mighty liner began to list, and as the lifeboats pulled away the orchestra played "Nearer, My God, to Thee." The ship trembled, turned slowly on her side, and disappeared, dragging down those who had not leaped overboard in the last moments. A very few were picked up by life-boats, most of which were too far off to attempt rescues or too fearful to take the risk. An unruffled sea, with only a bit of ship's furniture and wreckage here and

there, gave no answer to the cries of the drowning or
the groans of the living. As the first tinge of dawn
lightened the scene, a gigantic iceberg floated majes-
tically out of view beyond the horizon.

Meanwhile, amid the excitements of political upheaval and disasters and crimes, the advance of industry

A foreign plant—Cologne, Germany.

had been uninterrupted. The keynote of that progress,
as economists and manufacturers came to realize, was
mass production, with Ford leading the way.

He had replaced his Piquette Avenue plant, in Detroit, with the Highland Park plant, covering sixty
acres. Car prices were raised a trifle in 1909 and 1910
to pay for this, the largest automobile factory in the
world. At the higher prices he sold 18,664 cars in a
year. Then he reduced the touring car to $780 and sold
34,528. Lowering prices whenever possible, raising them
only when necessary, was the Ford watchword. The
business had spread afar, with plants at London and
Australia and shipments to every quarter of the globe.

Manufacturing methods had improved steadily, owing to constant experimenting, and to the discovery of new and better ways to make the thousands of parts of Model T. (The present Ford V-8 has 15,000 parts.) What was needed in the new plant was a system by which mass production would proceed at the highest speed, with the maximum of order and coördination in an army of workmen.

Gradually the assembly line, the basis of economical production in the Ford plants, grew into an institution. It is now imitated in all the large manufacturing industries of the world, though the imitators have not always echoed Ford's insistence that mass production must be "flexible," with unceasing reduction of costs in order to sell goods for lower prices.

To take the work to the men, rather than the men to the work, was the basic idea of the assembly line. Heretofore workers had fallen over each other as they searched for tools and materials. Ford had been attacking by degrees the every-fellow-for-himself relic of factory traditions. He now formulated his ideas for putting an end to haphazard methods. First, he specified, all tools and men should be in the sequence of the operation, so that each part or material would travel the least distance in the finishing processes. Second, mechanical carriers must be provided, upon which each workman would drop a completed part, to be carried to the next man for his operation. Third, sliding assembly lines should deliver the parts at convenient distances. One movement for one man, a reduction of the necessity of thought and of unnecessary movements by the workers, was the aim of the new system.

To an observer untrained in technicalities, a group of assembly lines is something like a network of railways, with the various branches feeding the main division. Along moving platforms and carriers travel processions of parts. The workmen stand at their appointed places, each with his one job, ranging from the placing of a tiny bolt to the fitting of a completed body on the chassis. Piece by piece the car grows until it passes off the final line under its own power. Each year brings improvements, saving a minute's time or a cent's cost, in the assembly line. In the Ford factory invention never ceases. If there is one tradition in this organization which does not believe in traditions, says the founder, it may be phrased as follows:

"Everything can always be done better than it is being done."

The origin of the assembly line at Highland Park, involving years of tests, illustrates the Ford method of moving forward. The initial experiment, in the spring of 1913, was made in assembling the flywheel magneto. It was a small experiment. Every novelty is tested by Ford in a small way, to make sure that the new method is better than the old. The general idea of the assembly line had come from the overhead trolley used by Chicago packers in dressing beef, but that was a simple mechanism by comparison with what the motor maker had in mind.

Having demonstrated in the next twelve months that the flywheel magneto could be assembled by a group of men in 13 minutes and 10 seconds, instead of the 20 minutes used by a single workman, Ford installed new lines for one operation after another. Soon he was moving the chassis down a track 250 feet long, drawing it along with a rope and windlass. Six men walked beside it, picking up parts from piles placed at intervals. The time of assembling the chassis was soon reduced from 12 hours and 8 minutes to 5 hours and 50 minutes. The height of the moving line was fixed at average waist level after many experiments. The speeds at which different lines traveled were changed until each workman had exactly the time he needed for his assigned task—not a second too much time nor a second too little. Finally the whole car was assembled by the same system.

In due course every line was mechanically driven. The workmen who attached screws, bolts, and nuts, or put on wheels, hub caps, and mudguards, or poured gasoline into the finished engine, or fastened the body to the chassis, stayed at their appointed places and received their parts from the department of transportation established for the purpose. No worker on the line moved or lifted anything; the thing he had to handle was brought to him and placed where he could pick it up without a wasted motion or a lost moment.

The idea of the assembly lines has not changed since 1914, though uncounted economies and accelerations have brought them nearer and nearer to perfection. Long ago the company duplicated the system in its plants scattered over the world; today River Rouge, successor of the Highland Park factory, turns out complete cars only for the Detroit district, though still making most of the parts shipped to the branch assembly plants.

How the new method saves time and money is shown

by the connecting-rod assembly, a tiny operation which required only about three minutes under the old system. Twenty-eight men used to sit at 2 benches, assembling 175 connecting rods in 9 hours. The foreman made a study of the workers' procedure with a stop-watch and found that they spent 4 hours in walking. He tried dividing the group into 3 divisions, placing a slide on a bench, 3 men at each side, and an inspector at the end. One man now performed only that part of the operation he could finish without shifting his feet. The squad was cut from 28 to 14, and a few years afterward to 7 men, who complete 2,600 assemblies in 8 hours. And as the number of men on each operation decreased, the number of men employed in the plant increased. Manufacturing economies resulted in larger business which in turn required more men.

Hand operations ceased long ago in the Ford plants wherever a machine could be made automatic, although only about 10 per cent of the tools are specially designed and the others are regular machines adjusted to their special jobs.

Ford does not believe in titles or fixed authority. Any worker may go over the head of his immediate boss with suggestions or complaints, but the privilege is not often used as the foremen know that justice is a requisite for holding their places. When a man is hired, nobody asks him for a testimonial; he may have a prison record, for all Ford cares. The only thing that matters is his fitness for work. To keep his job he must work, and promotion is at hand for those who can do especially well what they have to do. The men in important posts—in another company they would be called by this or that imposing title—have risen from the bottom; but Ford has said that a small percentage of wage-earners take advantage of opportunities to rise into higher positions, as most of them avoid the added labor and responsibilities which promotion entails. He has found that he always needs men who are able and willing to take difficult jobs, while the majority prefer work of the repetitive kind afforded by the assembly line, doing the same thing over and over, day after day. The opportunities for men of extra intelligence and skill have increased with each year's improvement in machines; inventive genius continues to provide machines which can do jobs better than human hands can accomplish similar results.

Answering the critics who say that monotony in a worker's movements is injurious to health, the manufacturer cites the case of one man who spent his days stepping on a treadle release. He underwent a physical examination to show whether he was becoming one-sided, learned that he was not, and yet was shifted to another job. Soon he asked that he be returned to his old place. Frequent inquiries by doctors in the Ford plants have failed to show any bodily abnormality caused by repetitive motions. When the men ask to be shifted to another kind of work, they are moved as soon as possible. For the most part they resist transfers.

Among the thousands of jobs, nearly half can be filled by persons of no great physical strength or stamina; many are held by cripples, and a few by blind men. The employment department decides where to use an applicant, whose course thereafter depends on himself. There have even been experiments with bedridden men, who in their periods of recuperation from accident or illness screw enough nuts on small bolts to earn their full wages before leaving the hospital. Their production has been actually above the shop average. None of them was required to do the work. They asked for it and seemed to recover more rapidly because they were busy.

Cleanliness, ventilation, and plenty of light are requisites of a Ford plant, where the machines, though placed closer together than in other factories, are arranged scientifically so as to give a worker exactly the space he needs. Every machine must be safe. Accidents are few, but after each one there is an inquiry as to methods to prevent that mishap from happening again. The Ford ideal is to make all machines foolproof. No new contrivance is installed until it is thoroughly tested.

While the assembly line was having its genesis, in 1913, this country was entering upon a vital period. A Democratic Administration moved into Washington, with advanced notions of running human affairs, after long years of conservative leadership. In Mexico a new President, Francesco I. Madero, was assassinated. Events in Europe were shaping themselves for the war crisis, though nobody yet realized it, least of all those who attended the dedication of the Peace Palace at The Hague. Raymond Poincaré, who was to hold his post through the war, became President of France. The death of J. Pierpont Morgan the elder and the preliminaries of founding the new Federal Reserve banking system, under Wilson's guidance, were the year's milestones in financial circles.

Not yet could it be said that Henry Ford was known throughout America. He had, of course, the attention of the automobile industry, which had undergone the painful experience of watching him disprove its maxims and scorn its extravagances, and he was doubtless appraised as a deliverer by thoughtful persons among half a million Model T owners, now able to explore far places instead of staying at home. Among manufacturers, in so far as his methods were discussed, he was regarded with curiosity, even suspicion. But only in his own neighborhood and among the few who studied his activities at close range was he looked upon as a national leader in business. Probably the greatest glare of publicity he had ever attracted was the advertising he sought deliberately in his racing years, when an unbelieving public refused to consider motorcars as serviceable vehicles and was interested in them only as speed machines. At the end of 1913 there were certainly many Americans who had never heard of Ford.

One week later his name was a household word. On January 5, 1914, came the announcement that the Ford Motor Company would pay a minimum wage of $5.00 a day, increasing the workers' average pay from $2.40. At the same time the day's work was cut from 9 to 8 hours. A month after the depression arrived, Ford increased his minimum wage from $6.00 to $7.00, which remained in force until September, 1931, when the previous minimum of $6.00 was resumed and worldwide depression had made the higher rates impossible.

The commotion caused in the newspapers and in business circles by the revolutionary move would be hard to exaggerate. Ford became the topic of innumerable articles in the daily press and the magazines, whereas previously the items about him were inconspicuous notes on his motor ideas, his factory standardization, and his stand in the Selden patent case. The effect of his methods on the business life of the country had been tremendous for years, but his emergence into the limelight that has since surrounded him was caused by the news that he would divide with his employees in the ensuing year a sum aggregating $10,000,000.

The wage increase was in effect a profit-sharing plan. Other manufacturers, though not a large proportion of them, had adopted the sharing principle of giving to the workers some part of the assured profits at the end of a year, but Ford's idea was different; he proposed to estimate profits in advance and pay the employees' share in the form of regular wages.

While the editors of the country accorded to him the treatment that is meted out to each new hero of the hour, finally chasing the naturally democratic inventor into a seclusion necessary for the conduct of his affairs, the conservatives of industry and the stockholders of his own company made no secret of their indignation. Such a wild scheme would destroy profits, they said. The stockholders, mindful of lessened dividends after the diversion of $10,000,000 to other pockets, tried to stop the controlling owner, just as they had endeavored to prevent him from concentrating on a useful car. Reactionary editorial articles dwelt upon the impossibility of carrying on business with such lavish expenditures. Rivals found consolation in predictions of bankruptcy for the innovator. This was a habit Ford's competitors had contracted long ago, and it had grown on them with each new stage of his unorthodoxy.

In the seven days before the plan went into effect a rush of unemployed laborers converged on Detroit, and the police had to drive away a mob from the gates of Highland Park. A smaller crowd of journalists, no less enthusiastic in seeking interviews than were the hordes looking for jobs, flocked into the city, delving into the personal life of the manufacturer, resurrecting the smallest incidents of his career, speculating on his intentions, trying to ferret out his relatives and friends for intimate talks, and making his existence less pleasant than it had been before he became a public character. When he made a trip to New York City, he found a crowd following him, a thousand or more letters waiting at his hotel, and headlines screaming his presence. A guard had to be established around his hotel rooms. But he submitted to a mass interview without protest, while the photographers snapped his every gesture.

Returning home after three days in the East, he proceeded to carry out his project, disregarding objections from inside or out. He had said that raised wages would result in lowered cost for his cars, and he proceeded to prove it.

In order to make sure that the men receiving the windfall would not become wasteful and cocksure, after the usual manner of those who grow suddenly prosperous, he founded a welfare department, which he explained was designed to teach his men how to prevent "sharpers" from taking their new gains away from them. The minimum wage was to be regarded as a bonus, and those entitled to its benefits must prove they ought to have it. Having decided that a business was made more secure by higher wages, but that a workman must be worth five dollars a day to get that much, he prescribed at the beginning that the bonus should go to married men living with their families and taking proper care of them, to single men of thrifty habits over twenty-two years old, and to younger men and women responsible for the support of next of kin.

Building for the indefinite future was the aim. Better work would be done by the worker who was surrounded by better living conditions and behaved himself consistently. Investigators proceeded to keep watch on the 14,000 Ford workers. Immediately 60 per cent qualified to share the profits, and the percentage increased to 78 in six months and 87 in a year. Changes have been made in the system, including stoppage of the inspector system after Ford made clear what kind of employees he wanted; but the principle of profit sharing through wage increases has endured. And the company's profits have been larger, in good or bad times, under the policy of paying as high wages as its treasury permitted.

It has been said by current historians that the "Ford joke" was born in 1914. The stories of the serviceable car, so unadorned and yet so permanent, must have been as numerous as the cars themselves. A book of them was collected and sold widely. Probably these jests were as good advertising as the most expensive displays; certainly they made no dent in Model T's record of success. Ford himself enjoyed them. It is related that occasionally he originated a story and turned to his advantage the popular habit of caricaturing his invention. One day he was traveling westward from New York in a fine English automobile, a Lanchester. A small procession of his associates followed. In the line were a

Packard and several Fords—which was not unusual, in view of the fact that every year the Ford company has bought models of all cars on the market, to study them and learn whatever lessons were to be got from their construction. A reporter along the route asked the inventor how it happened that he was not driving a Ford car.

"I am on a vacation," he replied. "We are in no hurry to get anywhere. That's why I'm not in a Ford."

In 1914 the building of concrete roads in the United States increased by more than a thousand miles, auguring a sixteen-year period of progress to the maximum construction of more than ten thousand miles annually. That was the year of the great fire in Salem, Massachusetts, when a thousand buildings were destroyed; the death of George Westinghouse, and the accession of Pope Pius X in succession to Benedict XV. All the happenings of the period, even the Ford wage change, were in the background of public attention before the year passed. While it seemed during the "period of neutrality" that the United States might avoid taking part in Europe's war and all our industries gained momentum, along with the automobile business, the public thought and talked war. Although the march of science and mechanics was apparently encouraged rather than hindered by the slaughter of human beings overseas, and jobs were plentiful in the land of the free, there hung over our prosperity a nagging fear, a terrifying uncertainty of what the future might bring.

V

WARTIMES AND AFTERWARD

THE Austrian Archduke Ferdinand and his wife were assassinated on June 28, 1914, at Sarajevo, in Bosnia; a Yugoslav student, brooding over the oppression of his country by Austria, started the flame that was to devastate Europe. A month afterward the Hapsburg monarchy declared war on Servia, and within six days Germany had invaded Belgium, and Russian armies were marching on Germany. England's decision to join France and Belgium followed. Early in August the German host, apparently irresistible, captured Liége, occupied Brussels, bombarded Louvain, and started toward Paris. With the first British troops in France, and Japan formally entering the war with the Allies, the Germans were halted only at the first Battle of the Marne, September 6th to 10th, and driven back to dig in for four years of trench fighting.

In October the cables described the fall of Antwerp, and in November the gruesome story of the first Battle of Ypres and the capture of the marauding cruiser *Emden* in the Pacific. Meanwhile, before the war started, United States marines had landed in Vera Cruz, Mexico, forecasting troubles which were to keep us occupied for years. Foreign entanglements, however, were not yet of sufficient importance to alarm the government at Washington, and President Wilson organized his Federal Reserve banks and issued his proclamation of neutrality.

With our peaceful course charted, we saw the Panama-Pacific International Exposition opened at San Francisco in 1915, the Federal Trade Commission founded, and the government railroad started in Alaska. From Europe that spring came news of British victories in the North Sea, the genesis of the German submarine blockade, the second Battle of Ypres, where poison gas was first used, and Italy's decision to take sides against Germany and Austria, her former treaty partners. For this country the sinking of the *Lusitania* off the Irish coast by a German torpedo, on May 7th, with the loss of 1,195 lives, was a forecast that the United States would not stay out of the war, though efforts continued at Washington to persuade the Germans to discontinue sinking ships with Americans on board. The following autumn saw the landing of British troops at Salonica and the execution of Edith Cavell, an English nurse, by the invaders in Belgium.

As if Providence were giving a demonstration of disasters in competition with man-made war, earthquakes killed 30,000 persons in central Italy, and our people had their attention diverted from overseas horror when the picnic steamboat *Eastland* turned turtle at Chicago with a loss of 812 passengers.

The millionth Ford car was produced at Highland Park on December 10, 1915. Production increased there and in the branch plants that were opened as sales mounted.

Through 1916 the war of stalemate dragged on—the Battle of Verdun, an uprising in Dublin, the consequent execution of Sir Roger Casement and other leaders, the arrival of a German submarine at Norfolk, the sea battle of Jutland, the third Ypres slaughter, the sinking of the *Hampshire* with Lord Kitchener aboard, two great battles on the river Somme, and the elevation of Lloyd George to be Prime Minister of Great Britain. Five days before Christmas a peace note by President Wilson was published, without effect.

Our troubles in Mexico had reached a climax, Villa raiding the New Mexico town of Columbus on March 9th, Pershing leading a punitory military expedition across the Border a few days later, and an agreement with Mexico resulting six months afterward, whereby the soldiers marched back over the Rio Grande. Politics that autumn were bitter. Wilson, with the campaign slogan "He kept us out of war," barely defeated Charles E. Hughes for the Presidency; the margin was a few hundred votes in California, where Hughes had offended the Republican Progressives, after winning the party nomination despite the antagonism of Theodore Roosevelt. Accomplishments of the year by the Wilson Administration included the Eight-Hour Railway Wage Law and the Workmen's Compensation Act. Further echoes of the war were the bombing of a Preparedness Day Parade in San Francisco (because of which Tom Mooney, though many students of the case have doubted his guilt, is still in prison) and the fatal explosion at the Black Tom docks in Jersey City, on the border of New York harbor.

In the period of neutrality Henry Ford did what he could, as an individual and as the head of a business, to support the cause of peace. He was against war, and he did not care who knew it. So earnestly had he expressed his views in advertisements during 1915 that the vice president of his company, James Couzens, resigned. In December of that year, only a few days before the millionth Model T came out of the factory, he started across the Atlantic on his "peace ship," which was a demonstration that at least one manufacturer did not want profits from legalized wholesale murder. Ford's idea was to furnish a neutral point close to the battlefields where representative men and women of the opposing nations might get together, regardless of the red tape of diplomacy, to discuss means of restoring peace. He did not accomplish that end. Doubtless he expected only to make his point that the peace idea still existed on earth.

An index of the growth of the automotive industry was the passage of the Federal Aid Act, on July 11, 1916, providing $75,000,000 in appropriations to be distributed over the next five years for highway improvements in all parts of the country. The outlay by the government for that purpose was to be increased to $200,000,000 in the year after the war.

Germany began its unrestricted submarine warfare on February 1, 1917, and two days afterward the United States broke off diplomatic relations. Congress declared war on April 6th. In the meantime the Czar of Russia had abdicated, and the assistance the Allies received from Russia thereafter was negligible. The first American troops sailed for France in late June, and their first shot was fired four months later, while the training of armies on a huge scale began in all our states, with the aim of sending to Europe as many mil-

A Ford freight carrier on the Great Lakes.

Cargoes arriving at the River Rouge Plant.

"Eagle Boats" for the Government
These wartime craft were built ten miles from the water in the old Highland Park factory.

lion men as might be needed. The Bolshevists overthrew the Russian Republic in November, the Battle of Cambrai was fought in the same month, and in December the British captured Jerusalem, and the United States made its drastic move of taking control of all the railroads. Adoption of the selective conscription plan, a departure from the methods of our previous wars, met only scant opposition, so intent was the body of our population upon finishing the ghastly job now that we had undertaken it. An interlude in warlike activities was the submission of the Prohibition Amendment by Congress to the states.

Henry Ford, when his country entered the war, took the stand of most of the peace advocates. He offered every facility of his organization to the government, without profit. While his factories continued a limited production of cars and parts, most of his efforts went into war materials until the Armistice was signed in 1918. He made special delivery trucks and ambulances without having to learn about them, and he made many things to which he had not given a thought before. Liberty motors for airplanes, caissons, listening devices, steel helmets, and eagle boats for combating sub-

A finished "Eagle Boat."

marines were turned out in quantities, and the Ford laboratories were busy experimenting with armor plate and other inventions peculiar to war. The government insisted that the eagle boats be constructed with the utmost rapidity, but the work must not interfere with the production of other war implements. The first boat was launched in July, 1918, six months after the navy gave its order. Not a forging or a rolled beam was used except in the engines; the hulls were built entirely of sheet steel, in a factory covering thirteen acres, erected for the purpose.

While Ford had been experimenting with farm tractors since 1902, he did not produce them until wartime. The Allies' food emergency in 1917 caused him to send the first of these tractors to England. Officers of the British government later expressed doubt whether it would have been possible to meet the crisis without them. They were operated mostly by women, who plowed up golf courses and landed estates for the raising of crops, without taking men away from the battle-fronts.

As there were not enough draft animals in Britain to cultivate crops to replace foodstuffs sunk by German submarines, the British investigated power farming. Only steam tractors were known in England, and there were few of them; all the factories were busy making munitions and could not stop to produce farming machinery. Turning to Ford, after testing some experimental tractors made at his Manchester plant, the Lloyd George government sent a cable asking his help. He replied that he would lend his drawings of the tractors' plans, the manufacturing and assembling to be done in

England, and would ship as many men as were needed to get the work under way, with Charles E. Sorensen, the general superintendent of the Ford Motor Company, as director of the job. It was soon discovered that many of the necessary materials could not be got in England, so they had to be shipped from Detroit. The lowest price Ford could quote was $1,500 for a tractor that should have been delivered for $700 under normal conditions. Sorensen was apologetic over the seemingly exorbitant figure, but Lord Milner promptly asked for 5,000 machines. The contract was signed and fulfilled according to schedule, despite the problems encountered in shipping materials over the submarine-infested ocean.

So England was introduced to Ford tractors a year before this country. In the next decade the invention developed into a movable power plant used for all sorts of farm purposes; it plowed, harrowed, and reaped, threshed, ran grist mills and saw mills, pulled stumps, and in countless ways aided in lessening agricultural drudgery. Once, when the Detroit shops were shut down because of a coal shortage, Ford printed his Dearborn newspaper by using a tractor for power to make plates. By 1922 the special tractor factory was in full operation, and the "Fordson," as it was called, remained in popular use in European countries after Ford discontinued making it in the United States.

The career of the tractor, after its start as an aid in wartime, has led us ahead of our story. When the British were solving their immense difficulties back in 1918, the Ford plant was one of many sources of American assistance. With a year of intensive training behind them, American divisions captured St. Mihiel on September 13th, took their share in the Battle of the Meuse-

Argonne in the two months following, helped to break the Hindenburg Line, and joined in the forward march that caused Germany to sue for peace. Meanwhile, the Central Powers' effort to stave off defeat by making a treaty with the Bolshevists, by bombarding Paris with long-range cannon, and by their eleventh-hour rallies against the revived Allied armies, had gone for naught; in a distant Russian province, at Ekaterinburg, the new rulers of the Slav empire had officially murdered the Czar Nicholas II and his family; on the seas scores of vessels had been sunk in the final campaign of the submarines; in the United States the old ways of peace had disappeared, and our daily habits were remodeled to conform with such innovations as railway and fuel control, daylight saving, and the other concomitants of war.

A people wild with joy celebrated the Armistice on November 11th, after having indulged in a similar or even more noisy celebration four days earlier upon hearing a false report that the war had ended. Then began at once the nine-year period which has come to be known in retrospect as the era of post-war hysterics.

"Red scares," fostered often by those who should have had their feet more firmly on the ground, were the most violent manifestations of the times; as soon as one proved groundless (there never was any sound evidence that Bolshevist influence or propaganda was having a real effect in America), another arose; political parties accused each other of encouraging the menace of communism; sects and racial groups blamed one another for inciting radicalism.

The total American investment in automobile manufacturing, not including the factories making parts, accessories, bodies, and tires, was $1,015,443,338 in 1919. There were 7,000,000 passenger cars, and 72 per cent of them were closed types, a contrast to the previous decade, when nearly all of them had been open.

Ford went back to full production immediately after

The Henry Ford Hospital, Detroit.

the war, advanced his minimum wage to $6.00 a day in 1919, and earned a net income of $71,000,000 for his company in the year. About the same time the Henry Ford Hospital, in Detroit, which had been taken over by the government, was returned to him. The plans for this institution were as great a novelty in medical circles as had been the "universal" car in the motor industry. Ford announced that it was for neither the rich nor the poor, but for self-supporting persons in between; all the rooms would be equally desirable, the resident doctors would be forbidden to practise outside, and all patients would have examinations by a sufficient number of physicians to insure a correct diagnosis. There were many other novel ideas for the hospital, but after years of successful operation they have ceased to excite comment. Millions have been invested in the institution, which is not expected to yield a profit. That fact, too, is no longer a cause of talk. The enterprises which Ford conducts without profit, or with a loss, are so numerous that the news of them is now a commonplace.

It is difficult to realize that fifteen years ago the buyer of a Ford car paid extra for a self-starter, and that the average legal speed for automobiles in the United States was twenty miles an hour, the thirty-mile speed allowed by New York and California being exceptional. But in 1919 there were many conditions that now seem archaic. The beauty-parlor business was an embryo, and women who used rouge on their faces were viewed askance; probably anybody who had put paint on the fingernails would have been arrested, as were those females who dared to appear on Eastern bathing beaches without stockings. Very short skirts and very short hair were not yet in vogue for women, but they came a few years later.

There had been no successful tabloid newspaper until the *Daily News* was established in New York that summer, and the old fogies predicted its failure along with the other new things in the world. Nation-wide prohibition went into effect at the end of June, when the wartime anti-liquor law, enacted many months previously, became operative, bridging the gap until the Constitutional amendment should supersede it the following winter. Ty Cobb of Detroit was still the base-ball idol, and Babe Ruth a beginner.

No radios had been installed, and wireless was still used only for code messages and distress signals at sea. What were later called post-war manners, bringing down the wrath of the elders upon the rising genera-tion, had not come to be recognized as a widespread phenomenon, through the results of our returning sol-diers' experiences in France included a broadening free-ness of speech and the appearance of the "well-dressed young man" in a soft shirt with his evening clothes. He soon sent the tailcoat into almost complete banish-ment, while the young women were not much behind him in ridding themselves of the trappings of a more sedate age.

The year 1919 was the beginning of a decade of sen-sational flights in the air, many of them fatal. John Alcock and A. W. Brown made the first non-stop Atlantic crossing in June, from Newfoundland to Ire-land. A fortnight later the British dirigible *R-34* came from Scotland to Long Island and soon returned safely to England. In October the pioneer trans-continental flight was made by Lieutenants W. B. May-nard and Alexander Pearson.

Theodore Roosevelt had died early in the year, which before its close saw Woodrow Wilson's downfall as a national leader and his physical collapse under the strain of campaigning for the Versailles Treaty. Returning from the Peace Conference, which he had persuaded to adopt his League of Nations plan, he found a majority of the Senate adamant against the idea. When reserva-tions which he regarded as nullifying the League's in-fluence were insisted upon by the Senate, he decided to

make a tour of the country and stir up sufficient senti-
ment to force a back-down of his adversaries; but his
health was shattered, and he was unable to recover from
a sudden illness in Pueblo, Colorado. They took him
back to the White House, an invalid for life.

While parades of returning soldiery, arriving at intervals through the year, aroused echoes of the wartime
fervor, a series of labor disturbances contributed to the
spirit of unrest. The Boston police, seeking increased
pay to cover the rising cost of living, went on strike;
the city's mayor asked the state of Massachusetts for
help; Governor Calvin Coolidge ordered out the guards-
men, and in reply to a protest from Samuel Gompers
gave voice to his famous statement that there was "no
right to strike against the public safety by anybody,
anywhere, any time." That doomed the strike and
helped Coolidge on the way to the White House.

Amid the unrest of 1920 was fought the Presidential
campaign that ended with the election of Warren G.
Harding by a tremendous vote. The succeeding years,
through the depressed period of 1921, the better business of 1922, and the rush into prosperity in 1923, still
found the advance of industry a contrast to the nervousness of the people in mass. The "Red scares" reached
a climax in the Wall Street explosion, which seemed to
be an isolated outrage of no significance in relation to
Bolshevist propaganda. The Prohibition and Woman
Suffrage amendments were in effect. Assassinations in
European countries became frequent. The new Union
of Soviet Socialist Republics, organized in 1922, seemed
on the way to permanence, though the "capitalistic"
world persisted in thinking it a passing show. Mussolini,

The lowest-priced Ford, in 1922, $369.

A Ford welfare project in a small village.

assuming the dictatorship of Italy under the opposite theory of Fascism, was headed toward order and peace, while the prophets performed their usual function of forecasting the reverse of what eventually happened.

If there was one place where post-war readjustment went ahead uninterruptedly, in the belief that human existence was destined for improvement, however different it might be from the old times, that place was the headquarters of the Ford Motor Company. The Ford principle of confidence in progress was not jolted. Even the evil of war, said the manufacturer, had brought good results, in the betterment of machinery and the increase of new inventions. Men were thinking more, doing wonders with their brains, in the era of perplexity.

When he turned out his five millionth Model T on May 15, 1921, Ford could look back on accomplishments more diversified than any business leader the world had known. In progressing from the gasoline buggy with its one cylinder to the "universal car," with its four cylinders, self-starter, and practically unlimited durability, he had not only established the greatest of automobile plants at Highland Park and begun to build at River Rouge one which would be much larger, but he had put to the test thousands of new methods and devices for reducing manufacturing costs, simplifying plant procedure, and improving the condition of workingmen.

Continuing to make most of his engines and parts at the main factory, he had distributed his assembling plants far afield. To an increasing extent manufacturing also was being done at other plants, lessening freight costs and speeding deliveries to the thousands of sales agencies. Besides experimenting with new machines, developing the assembly line until it became the dominant idea of the plants, and multiplying the equipment for making everything he found he could make more economically than he could buy, he went into scores of feeder industries hitherto considered independent of the motor maker's province. He bought a glass factory and made glass better and cheaper than he could get it elsewhere; acquired forests to supply the wood used in his cars, dug his own coal in his own Kentucky mines, brought iron from his own ore lands in his own steamships, took over a railroad 350 miles long when its service to his main plants proved unsatisfactory, and collected numerous smaller establishments in which to manufacture what he needed.

From the first it had been his plan to buy whenever possible, to manufacture only when he could save money and improve quality, with the exception that he did not want anybody else to build his engines or assemble his cars. For fifteen years or more, beginning with the company's start in the rented Detroit carpenter shop, there was a steady increase in the number of things he made for use in his cars. Of late years, however, his outside purchases have been increasing. Today more than five thousand different concerns make articles for Ford, whereas a few years ago the number was below three thousand five hundred. No doubt his leadership in industrial economy and quality production is largely responsible for the fact that others can now do many of the things which he formerly was obliged to do for himself.

His interests by this time had led to outside activities which had no more direct bearing on motor-making than on any other business, but which he regarded as beneficial to human progress. Village industries and farming had concerned him for years. Gradually he enlarged his experiments in both. Describing one of the small plants he organized in southern Michigan, in line with his theory that centralization of manufacturing was destined eventually to yield to decentralization, he wrote:

> All the men live within a few miles of the plant and come to work by automobile. Many of them own farms or homes. We have not drawn men from the farms—we have added industry to farming. One worker operates a farm which requires him to have two trucks, a tractor, and a small closed car. Another man, with the aid of his wife, clears more than five hundred dollars a season on flowers. We give any man a leave of absence to work on his farm, but with the aid of machinery these farmers are out of the shops a surprisingly short while—they spend no time at all sitting around waiting for crops to come up. They have the industrial idea and are not content to be setting hens.
>
> Now that the plant is well in operation, we take only employees from the district and none at all from Detroit. The change in the country has been remarkable. With the added purchasing power of our wages, the stores have been made larger and better, the streets have been improved, and the whole town has taken on a new life. That is one of the ways in which the wage motive inevitably works out.

In the same region where these small plants flourish he has established experimental farms, altogether about forty thousand acres, where the practice of coöperative farming is tested under the owner's direction. In one of his advertisements in recent years he said:

For a long time I have believed that industry and agriculture are natural partners and that they should begin to recognize and practise their partnership. Each of them is suffering from ailments which the other can cure. Agriculture needs a wider and steadier market; industrial workers need more and steadier jobs. Can each be made to supply what the other needs? I think so.

The link between is chemistry. In the vicinity of Dearborn we are farming twenty thousand acres for everything from sunflowers to soy beans. We pass the crops through our laboratory to learn how they may be used in the manufacture of motorcars and thus provide an industrial market for the farmer's products. I foresee the time when industry shall no longer denude the forests which require generations to mature, nor use up the mines which were ages in making, but shall draw its raw material largely from the annual produce of the fields. The dinner table of the world is not a sufficient outlet for the farmer's products; there must be found a wider market, if agriculture is to be all that it is competent of becoming. And where is that market to be found if not in industry?

I am convinced that we shall be able to get out of yearly crops most of the basic materials which we now get from forest and mine. That is to say, we shall grow annually many if not most of the substances needed in manufacturing. When that day comes, and it is surely on the way, the farmer will not lack a market and the worker will not lack a job. More people will live in the country. The present unnatural condition will be naturally balanced again. Our foundations will be once more securely laid in the land.

The day of small industry near the farm will return, because much of the material grown for industry can be given its first processing by the men who raised it. The master farmer will become, as he was in former years, master of a form of industry besides. . . .

Our times are primitive. True progress is yet to come. The industrial age has scarcely dawned as yet; we see only its first crude beginnings.

When Ford celebrated his sixtieth birthday in 1923 by turning out 7,000 cars in one day, the first balloon tire had just been put on the market by Firestone. Car production was rushing into further millions every year. There were already 40,000 buses on the roads in this country. In the Ford headquarters, with an entirely new personnel under his direction now that his original associates had withdrawn, the inventor had reached a point where he could no longer devote himself wholly to the mechanical side of the company. His theories on finances and management, relations of capital and labor, had attracted worldwide attention in his recent autobiography, and were subsequently amplified in other volumes and various interviews.* One of his pronouncements which gave the public its first real conception of the company's resources in 1922 was this:

It has been our policy always to keep on hand a large amount of cash—the cash balance in recent years has usually been in excess of fifty million dollars. This is deposited in banks all over the country. We do not borrow, but we have established lines of credit, so that if we so cared we might raise a very large amount of money by bank borrowing. But keeping the cash reserve makes bor-

*Books by Henry Ford, written in collaboration with Samuel Crowther, are: *My Life and Work, Today and Tomorrow, Edison as I Know Him,* and *Moving Forward.*

rowing unnecessary—our provision is only to be prepared to meet an emergency. I have no prejudice against proper borrowing. It is merely that I do not want to run the danger of having the control of the business and hence the particular idea of service to which I am devoted taken into other hands.

The years between wartime and the boom period saw the birth of radio broadcasting. An officer of the Westinghouse Company in East Pittsburgh had started in 1920 to send out music and baseball scores in a haphazard fashion from his station in an old barn. Within two years—while the country's avocations continued to include movements for averting the Bolshevist menace, and the younger generation went in for the free-and-easy, and a large part of both generations adopted each new fad and fancy of the hectic times—the annual business of selling radio sets rose to $60,000,000. In another seven years it reached $842,000,000.

Other events of the four years ending with 1923 were the organization of the League of Nations, without our assistance; the establishment of the independent kingdom of Egypt under a British protectorate, and the proclamation of the Irish Free State. The grist of disaster included the wrecks of two dirigible balloons, the ZR-2 in England, and the *Roma* over Hampton, Virginia, and two earthquakes that killed 300,000 persons in Japan and China. Portuguese flyers made the first air crossing of the South Atlantic. The Washington Conference for the Limitation of Armaments was called by President Harding in 1921, the Lincoln Memorial dedicated at Washington in the next year. The last American troops were withdrawn from the Rhine, and

Calvin Coolidge became President after Harding's death, in 1923. There was a new Pope, Pius XI, in Rome. Two of the world's most glamorous figures passed away, Admiral Robert E. Peary in 1920 and Madame Sarah Bernhardt in 1923.

The ten millionth Model T came out of the Ford factory on June 4, 1924, when the business boom was under full swing, five months before Coolidge was re-elected President. The "universal car" had sold as high as $1,250 and as low as $250, and yet wages had gone up and up, in accordance with Ford's repeated insistence that a product wanted by a large proportion of the public could be made more cheaply by high-priced workers with economical methods. His critics were less vocal now, and the example he had set bore fruit in raised pay checks everywhere, without regard to the speculative boom which was beginning to set the scene for depression.

Rural concrete road mileage, less than five miles at the beginning of Model T's career, increased to 31,146 miles in 1924. The prices of commodities went higher as car prices fell. That contrast did not affect the general prosperity of industry, which with few exceptions moved forward steadily. Hopeful signs of the year were the acceptance of the Dawes Reparation Plan by the Allies and Germany, the beginning of a withdrawal of French troops from the Ruhr, and the appointment of Owen D. Young as agent of the scaled-down reparation payments. A United States army airplane made a trip around the world, with few stops. The dirigible *Los Angeles* flew from Friedrichshaven to New York. The death of Woodrow Wilson occurred early in the year.

Congress enacted a law restricting immigration and ex-cluding the Japanese, and passed the first Soldiers' Bonus Bill over President Coolidge's veto. The beauty-parlor business became one of the nation's most profitable in-dustries. Use of the radio spread until hardly a housetop lacked its aërial wire, after the deadlocked Democratic Convention in New York had shown how easy it was to follow news, hear speeches, and enjoy music over the air. The crossword puzzle craze was born, also the fashion of baggy trousers for bareheaded collegians. An American tour by the Prince of Wales delighted the crowd. Eleanor Duse, the great Italian actress, died. France chose a new President, Gaston Doumergue.

In 1925 the Ford Motor Company paid wages amounting to $250,000,000, and it was estimated that $500,000,000 went to the workers in outside factories serving the company, and another $250,000,000 to the sales forces, making a total of about $1,000,000,000 contributed to the public purse. Ford again called at-tention to the relation of cost and pay checks; the price of cars had decreased 40 per cent since 1913, when wages were only averaging $2.40 a day.

Everything else kept going up in cost. Letter postage rose to three cents. The people had the money to pay, and sellers were not lacking who made them pay more than the products were worth. Nearly every group of citizens except the farmers felt prosperous that year and for some time afterward.

The news of the world, which was beginning to be parceled out by radio broadcasters as well as newspapers (such news broadcasting continued without friction until these two machines of public information recently grew jealous and made a bargain to keep off each other's preserves), covered the wreck of a United States navy dirigible in a thunder squall, a series of fatal storms in the Middle West, an earthquake calamity in Japan, the signing of the Nine-Power Treaty, the ratification of the Locarno Pact, and the death of the foremost American portrait painter, John S. Sargent. The Persian shah was deposed, ending a dynasty which had ruled for 146 years. Greece proclaimed herself a republic. The Turks followed suit, abolishing polygamy by law and giving to their new president, Mustapha Kemal, the privilege of granting divorces, whereupon he immediately ordered one for himself. Siam got a new king, Prajadhipok, who a few years later made a visit to this country.

In order to make Model T a better car, Ford had eighty-one changes made in it. The most noticeable one in the public mind was a new body shape and hood, which, however, were not destined to be long in evidence. Model T's honorable and productive career was soon to end. The eighty-one changes cost the Ford company $1,395,596 for materials and $5,682,387 for labor. Other expenses raised the total to $8,000,000, without counting the time lost from production. That huge outlay was a small matter compared to what was to come when Model T went off the market. But a summary of the company's resources at the time shows even the largest operation could have had no terrors for Ford.

There were, in 1928, 86 Ford plants and branches, including those of the Ford Motor Company of Canada. Fifty-two were in the United States, 34 in other countries. Of the domestic factories, 17 were manufacturing plants and 35 were partly for assembling and partly for service. In that last year of full production, the capacity of the plants was 2,000,000 cars annually.

Total profits of the Ford Motor Company from 1903 to 1926, inclusive, were $900,839,000. In the nineteen

MODEL T—*The new shape of 1926.*

years of Model T, it paid out wages and salaries of nearly $2,000,000,000, not including 1918, when the factories were largely occupied with war work. The aggregate sum paid to those who contributed to Model T's manufacture, including the forces of companies selling supplies and parts to Ford, reached the extraordinary figure of $7,000,000,000. Even that was not the full amount, for it did not include the wages of train workers, oil and rubber laborers, and many others.

While the accumulation of the resources that made such outlays possible was due primarily to new inventions and improved methods of handling improved tools, economies in management played a large part. Among such economies none was more important, or more characteristic of Ford, than his war against waste. His idea of stopping waste included getting use, or value, out of things which had not been used or valuable before. His salvage department was earning at least $20,000,000 a year. It would take a whole book to tell all the savings. A few will suffice as examples: 80,000,-000 pounds of steel that once had gone into scrap were handled profitably each year. Uses were found for rags, scrap oil, old brick, paper, and fragments of wood. In shipping car bodies one freight car was used where formerly eighteen had been needed, because the bodies were not forwarded in pieces to be assembled in branch plants. On the vessels built to take materials and parts to European, South American, and Pacific Coast branches, the company saved $20,000 on every trip by loading "loose" the cargoes which once had been crated for railway transportation.

The most spectacular work of salvage was the tearing apart of 199 ships bought from the United States Shipping Board. From these steel vessels, which were "disassembled" at huge cost after special machinery had been manufactured for the task, a force varying from 1,000 to 1,500 men removed about 90,000 feet of wood, untold quantities of paper and beaver board, radiators, mouldings, hinges, locks, door knobs, brass and electrical fixtures, pumps, oil gauges, and other articles, and, of course, the larger item of several hundred tons of steel from each ship—all usable in the Ford scheme of things. The ships were bought for $1,697,470. Special equipment for the salvaging cost $1,000,000, and labor half a million. The profits on the undertaking, if

ASSEMBLY LINE—*Fitting the crankshaft in place.*

there were any, Ford never estimated. He said he was satisfied with the lesson he and his men learned.

We have on the credit side [he wrote] something that cannot be reduced to figures—we have the experience which our men gained in solving this big new problem. That is always a prime profit. The training we gained, the confidence, the new insight into methods, render me quite indifferent to anything that figures could show. In reckoning gains you must reckon the growing ability of your

ASSEMBLY LINE—*The engine installed.*

organization as far more important than a growing balance in the bank.

In listing his company's activities up to Model T's banner year, Ford mentioned the building of the Lincoln car, a more expensive automobile which was never intended to be a commodity, though it also has its interchangeable parts and is of standardized manufacture; the operation of iron and coal mines and lumber camps, the extension of the Fordson plant as a converter of raw materials and waste, the building of a laboratory at Dearborn, the worldwide system of branch factories, and the manufacture of glass, cement, flax, artificial leather, and chemical compounds. The necessity for entering other lines than automobile manufacture was evidenced, he pointed out, by the fact that only two of his various by-products were procurable outside the company.

The investment in the American automobile industry attained its peak in 1926, totaling $2,089,489,325, which was more than double what it had been seven years before, and American roads were being hard-surfaced at the rate of 40,000 miles annually at a cost of about $1,000,000,000.

The year was notable for crises in foreign affairs, labor disturbances, aëronautical exploits, and increased popular interest in sports of all sorts. The new Turkish régime made civil marriage obligatory, with religious

ASSEMBLY LINE—*Ready for the finishing touches.*

ceremonies optional; Germany was admitted to the League of Nations; Japan acquired a new emperor, Hirohito. An anthracite strike was settled after lasting six months; in England a general strike of 2,500,000

ASSEMBLY LINE—*Completed cars on their way out.*

workers was called off in nine days, but the miners stayed out for months afterward. Byrd crossed the North Pole in an airplane, and the Amundsen-Nobile expedition in a dirigible balloon followed three days later. In the summer the English Channel was full of swimmers trying for new records. Television was invented by J. L. Baird. A tropical hurricane raged across the Bahama Islands, Florida, Alabama, and Mississippi, causing most damage in Miami and the neighboring cities. Philadelphia had its Sesquicentennial Exposition. Two incidents which absorbed the attention of a large public were the American tour of Queen Marie of Rumania and the death of the motion-picture star Rudolph Valentino, at whose funeral women formed lines stretching nine blocks from a New York undertaking establishment.

After the fifteen millionth Model T came out of the factory in 1927, Henry Ford announced his decision to abandon the car which had ruled the roads for nineteen years. The time had arrived when refinements in automobile construction should be regarded as necessities; as the scale of living rose, it was logical that comfort in transportation should keep pace with the ever increasing comforts of living generally. In pace with the times Ford reached another conclusion; after experimenting with the five-day week for a year, he said he had demonstrated that the shorter period of labor increased production in his plants. He expressed the opinion that the five-day week should not be enforced by law, as some industries were not yet ready for it, but predicted that it would be generally adopted and that eventually the daily working shift could be profitably reduced below eight hours. Not less work, but better and more work in less time, with better methods and better tools, became a permanent Ford policy, without affecting the policies of higher wages and improved production.

VI
THE REBUILDING OF AN INDUSTRY

CHANGES IN THE FORD PLANTS for the production of a new model involved an expenditure of money and time almost beyond computation. The cost was more than a hundred million dollars. Nearly forty thousand machines were scrapped and new ones installed in their stead. The factories, except those making parts for Model T, were shut down for the alterations in the spring of 1927, when the plan was announced. On December 2d the new car was offered for sale in showrooms over the country.

For nearly twenty years Ford had been making changes, throwing out old machines and tools as he found better ones, and these gradual replacements had furnished experience for the gigantic shift of 1927. The previous alterations in shop equipment had not interrupted production, as it had been arranged in each case, when the improving of a part was contemplated, simply to make greater quantities of that part than were needed and to use the oversupply while the substitution of new machinery was effected in a section of the plant. But the wholesale recasting of the business to change from Model T to Model A meant rearranging and replacing all the machinery at once and a consequent stoppage of production.

So the industry was remade from top to bottom. Decreasing the working forces by nearly twenty-five thousand men resulted, but Ford, while regretting this necessity, voiced the prediction that in the long run the revamping would provide jobs for more men than ever before—which within two years proved to be the case. He also expressed the opinion that a company which feared to make improvements in its methods and product, however costly, would eventually reach a point where it could not employ anybody at all.

The major decision when the transformation began, just after the fifteen millionth Model T had been turned out, was to develop the River Rouge Plant into the main factory, replacing Highland Park as the largest automobile center in existence. To Highland Park was assigned the manufacture of parts for the old models, of which tens of thousands would remain on the roads for years to come.

Not only were new machine tools installed for use in constructing Model A, but the whole power plant at Highland Park was abandoned, and at River Rouge were set up turbogenerators giving 250,000 horsepower, more than twice the amount used before. Other major machinery which could have continued to serve its purpose was replaced by more modern inventions; in short, Ford took advantage of the shut-down to revise every phase of factory equipment capable of improvement and did not confine his betterments to those implements which must be changed in order to make a new model.

For example, the largest power press in the Model T régime, weighing about two hundred thousand pounds, gave place to presses of five hundred thousand pounds or more. In making the old car there had been a tend-

The World's Largest Automobile Plant, at River Rouge

(Insert) Ford's First Brick Factory in Detroit.

ency to increase welding. The new one was to be composed 90 per cent of steel, with a minimum of cast parts.

> We could in most instances have fitted our new design to the existing machinery [wrote the manufacturer, in describing the operation] but that would not have been as economical in the end as disregarding our machinery and taking a fresh start. The new machinery is in line with future progress. It pays in the end to do a thing right.

Machines and men from every department at Highland Park were shifted. Equipment was shipped to assembly plants in other parts of the country and overseas. The layouts of plants were remapped, new buildings erected from foundation to roof. In the early autumn, while the public was being regaled with daily rumors about the new model, partial production of the car was under way. The final assembly line was moved from Highland Park to River Rouge. The new plant, covering two square miles, soon contained nearly thirty miles of conveyors. Departments transferred from Highland Park included those which made roller bearings, ball bearings, axle shafts, gears, wheels, die castings, radius rods, and universal joints. A study of space-saving resulted in a reduction of the area occupied by the final assembly line by one half, without decreasing the output, and a reorganization of eighteen departments into fourteen occupying nearly 10 per cent less floor room.

Minute plans for each moving operation were prepared in advance. First, the men charged with the relocation checked every inch of space allotted for a

department in the River Rouge Plant. Then came the
workmen, who, while waiting for their machines to
follow, were placed temporarily in whatever space was
available near their pre-arranged stations. Heavy machines were transported in railroad flat cars, lighter ones
in trucks. All the while, builders were busy on new
construction, electricians were hitching up machines

MODEL A—*After the recasting of the Ford industry.*

to the power lines, and an army of inspectors was
checking each of the innumerable details.

What was going on at River Rouge was happening
to a lesser degree in the tributary plants around the
world.

The first Model A came off the assembly line on
October 20th. It was a far cry from its predecessor, and
had an up-to-date body shape, more room inside, a
gear shift like that of the expensive automobiles, and

was painted in a variety of colors to suit all tastes. In the hood was no line reminiscent of the famous Model T. When the new cars were displayed on the second day of December, they afforded a first-page sensation for the daily newspapers. Crowds jammed the streets around city showrooms, and the police had to be called to keep order. It was estimated that a million persons tried to see the new model in New York. For months previously there had appeared columns of speculations as to what Ford was doing, to what extent he would change the appearance of his "universal car" and its mechanism, and whether his policies of low prices and high wages would continue to keep him in the lead.

Eleven months later the production reached 6,000 cars a day, which were enough to start Model A on the way to paying back at least a part of the cost it had entailed; 186,313 men were employed by the company, and wages were still up and prices still down.

In the meantime, the automobile business centering at River Rouge was not the only phase of American life to undergo radical changes. Something had happened to improve the public's temper and increase its optimism, at least as far as the younger generation was concerned. In the opinion of thoughtful observers there was evident about this time a lessening of the race after bizarre fads and an increase of attention to education and work. Though the older generation, set in its ways, was immersed in the speculative mania that was to reach a climax so soon, the young men and women seemed to be outgrowing the nervousness of the postwar era. The causes of this were probably so various as to be a topic of debate rather than proof, but many

analysts of current events have fixed on a single incident as marking the transition.

A young man with a shock of blond hair and an
engaging gravity of manner flew an airplane from St.
Louis in the spring of 1927, stayed a few days on Long
Island among crowds that paid little attention to him,

Henry Ford and Charles A. Lindbergh.

and on May 20th took off toward the Atlantic Ocean.
On the following day, while the world marveled, its
attitude of indifference now replaced by the wildest
enthusiasm, the lone flyer hovered and circled over
Paris and glided down to the aviation field of Le
Bourget.

"I am Charles Lindbergh," he said to the vanguard of an immense throng closing around his snow-white plane.

Others had flown the Atlantic. At that moment a score of more experienced but less determined pilots were waiting for better winds and fairer weather to try for the $25,000 prize which had gone unearned since a Frenchman resident on Fifth Avenue offered it six years previously for the first direct flight from New York to Paris. Several of them were to duplicate the Lindbergh feat, and flights of greater distances were to be accomplished, but without dimming the fame of the quiet youth from the Middle West.

Lindbergh the unknown became overnight the hero of the generation. After he had made a short tour of European capitals, with crowds and kings alike striving to do him honor, and when he returned home to a welcome beyond the dreams of conquerors, the hero-worship continued with a unanimity that would have been incredible if it had not been so completely proved. There had been no such instance of idolatry in our times.

Looking back from the vantage of later years, one wonders at the phenomenon of such a united public opinion in a period which otherwise was distinctive for its conflicting views and prejudices. Perhaps the explanation is that a floundering world, worn out by the tensions and uncertainties of nearly a decade since the war, needed a sudden emotional experience to bring back its sense of balance. At any rate, the millions of our citizens took Lindbergh to their hearts, and he became the ideal for a new generation which had been growing up in an atmosphere of fear, cynicism, and frivolity.

It was a banner year for transoceanic aërial adventures, whether or not the flights had any permanent effect on the promotion of practical and safe air travel. Two Frenchmen, Nungesser and Coli, had tried to make the journey westward from Paris to New York, but had disappeared, nobody knew where. Two weeks after the Lindbergh achievement Clarence D. Chamberlin, flying with Charles A. Levine as backer and passenger, soared from New York to Eisleben, Germany, breaking all distance records. Commander Richard E. Byrd and three companions followed in another fortnight, landing in the surf off the French shoreline. Ruth Elder and George Haldeman started from New York in the fall, dropped into the sea near the Azores, and were rescued by a passing steamship. As the year ended, Mrs. Frances W. Grayson and three others left Ireland in a hydroplane and were lost. Other fatal attempts, leaving no traces of the flyers' fate, had been those of Paul Redfern, who started from Brunswick, Georgia, for Brazil; Princess Lowenstein-Wertheim, lost with three associates on the way from London to New York; Philip D. Payne and two friends swallowed up in the unknown on their way from Maine to Italy, and Captain Jerry Tully and Lieutenant James Metcalf, trying to fly from Newfoundland to London.

Radio broadcasting grew into such an institution in the year that the Federal Radio Commission was created, and sales of receiving sets increased to $400,000,-000, a sum that was to be doubled in the next two years. Other events of 1927 were the Mississippi River floods, which inundated 20,000 square miles in six states and were followed by tornadoes that swelled the property losses to a quarter of a billion dollars; the sending of our marines to Nicaragua, for the usual purpose of protecting American interests, and the civil war in China, where the marines had their innings along with 15,000 soldiers from other nations. There were more than 64,000 miles of federal aid roads finished in the year. The tide of prosperity rose steadily.

All the government had to do in those days, it appeared, was to sit by and watch good times get better. In 1928, when boom days reached their apex, about half a million Americans traveled to foreign countries, most of them on pleasure bent. When they came home, they left $650,000,000 behind them, an appreciable part of it spent on fine raiment. With money plentiful and the radio spreading news of Paris fashions to every hamlet and farm, the American tourists were no longer confined to the city-bred. They came from the far corners, and the country cousins were as numerous as the city sisters, and quite as knowing, when it came to invading the French shops.

When the end of the boom period rolled around, in 1929, Model A had taken the lead in the sales of motorcars. Ford was still unique among manufacturers in that he bothered himself no more than the necessity of the moment demanded and was troubled not at all by pessimism over the future. When times began to be less prosperous, he fell back on his philosophy that the market for a serviceable product could not be disturbed for long, and that the millions he had spent for making over his factories, or might continue to spend for recovery, were investments in the future rather than losses to be lamented. He kept on spending. Soon after the reconstruction of the factories, he made one of his largest investments in entering the Brazil rubber field, purchasing vast tracts, and instituting an experiment of indefinite magnitude for the purpose of providing a rubber supply independent of European and Asiatic markets.

His response to the stock-market crash in the fall of 1929 was to announce on December 1st an increase of the minimum wage to $7.00 a day, which would involve annual payment of an additional $20,000,000 by the company. In a few months his payrolls showed that the workers were receiving an average rate of $1.00 an hour, which was as much as an unskilled laborer earned in a ten-hour day early in 1910, the year after Model T went on sale. In the twenty years manufacturing costs had decreased so much, owing to economic methods, that the cost of fine materials used in motor building was less than half of what comparatively crude materials had cost in 1910. Better and better machines had given men more and more jobs, with less drudgery, as the years passed.

The road transportation boom found twenty-three million passenger automobiles registered in the United States in 1929, and the production value of the motor industry exceeded three and three quarters billion dollars. Motor vehicles on farms numbered more than five millions, including nearly a million trucks. The gasoline engine had revolutionized our mode of life in city and country, and it was estimated that motor users were paying special taxes of about a billion dollars annually.

Of the nearly three million miles of highways in the United States, more than fifty thousand miles were built of concrete.

Through 1928-29 adventuring in air navigation had continued, and the exploits, many of them fatal, had an effect on the aviation industry in some measure comparable to the influence racing had exerted on motor building in the early days. In April, 1928, a westward voyage over the Atlantic was made for the first time in the plane *Bremen*, carrying Captain Koehl, Captain Fitzmaurice, and Baron von Huenefeld. Sir George H. Wilkins reached eight-four degrees north latitude by plane in the same week, and a few weeks later General Nobile of Italy took a dirigible across the North Pole. Amelia Earhart, as a passenger, was the first woman to fly the Atlantic, from Newfoundland to Wales. A non-stop flight from Italy to Brazil was made by Ferrarin and Del Prete. Byrd, having started in 1928 on the first Antarctic expedition, used the airplane extensively, flying over the South Pole in a Ford plane and returning home in 1930. The German dirigible *Graf Zeppelin*, Captain Eckener commanding, led the way in ocean crossing with a lighter-than-air passenger vehicle and has since repeated the achievement several times. Lindbergh, devoting himself to aviation as a business and still holding his popularity (except with a small number of news gatherers, whom he offended by showing a disinclination to encourage personal publicity), made a good-will tour to Latin America in 1928 and has undertaken a number of notable explorations since, with never a mishap and often with his wife as a flying partner. Flights of 1929 included that of a Spanish plane, bearing Jiminez and Iglesias, from Seville to Brazil, and the voyage of Lotti, Assolant, and Lefevre in a French craft from Old Orchard Beach to Spain.

The inauguration of Herbert Hoover as President in

AT THE EDISON CELEBRATION IN 1929
Left to right: Francis Jehl, Thomas A. Edison, President Hoover, and Henry Ford, in the renovated Edison Laboratory at Dearborn.

1929, after he had sought a rest from the labors of the political campaign by touring the Latin-American republics, was celebrated in the midst of what seemed on the surface to be a continuation of prosperous times; but the forces that soon brought financial disaster and social upheaval were already making themselves felt. Not the least of the country's troubles was the growth of gangster depredations in the large cities.

The year was marked by frequent prison mutinies, showing the inadequacy of quarters for the increasing number of inmates and the weakness of laws designed to solve the question of crime.

For the relief of the farmers, who had not benefited from the good times like most other groups, the Federal Farm Board was established soon after Hoover entered the White House. In foreign relations the peace effort resulting in the Kellogg-Briand Anti-War Treaty, pledging sixty-two powers to refrain from war as an instrument of national policy, seemed a notable achievement. The new Prime Minister of Great Britain, Ramsay MacDonald, came to Washington to talk about naval armaments with President Hoover. The Russian Soviet government, in the meanwhile, had settled itself under the dictatorship of Stalin and announced its five-year plan of industrial and agricultural development, involving an investment of thirty-three billion dollars, an increase of 133 per cent in the country's industrial output, and a 55 per cent increase in agricultural production. Italy and the Pope had made peace after half a century. The Turks had abandoned Islam as their official religion, and the throne of Afghanistan had been abdicated by three kings in a single year, leaving the fourth in uncertain occupancy.

The year 1930, while it brought no joy to the speculators and their families, as they saw paper profits dwindling and stock-market quotations falling toward their ultimate depth of fifty billion dollars below the boom peak, found Henry Ford distinctly on the up-grade. Three years after the great change in his plants, he was employing more men than ever before. The motor-making business in general held its gains. Taxes were growing, which did not sound well to the students of economics; out of every dollar spent for gasoline, thirty cents was a tax. Yet the optimistic citizen, as the evidences of bad times accumulated, said prosperity still lingered just around the corner. There were few who believed in the depression until they met it in person. In the automobile industry the very fact of rising taxes had a flattering connotation, when the statisticians discovered that motor-vehicle users were paying 18 per cent of the nation's levies on property valued at five and a half billion dollars while the railways paid only one and four-tenths per cent of the taxes on property appraised at twenty-five billions. That might seem unjust, but at least it indicated that the automobiles were doing their big bit to keep the government going.

Ford's optimism, as the reader will have observed long since, was of the chronic variety and was not based on vain hopes. His records showed that he won success in bad years as well as good ones. There had not been a time when his cars failed to sell. In 1930 he was proceeding as confidently as before.

We have now reorganized our companies in England, Germany, France, and other countries, recapitalized them on a very conservative basis, and sold the stock in each company to the citizens of the country in which it is situated [he wrote that year]. We retain the control of each company only so that it may be managed in accordance with our fundamental principles and have the benefit of our engineering experience. We are not at all interested merely in floating a number of automobile companies in Europe or anywhere else in the world. But we believe that our industrial policies move toward the end of creating consuming power, raising the standards of living, and thus diminishing poverty. In this belief we may be right or again we may be wrong—we believe that our experience has proved we are right.

In Russia a different course was being pursued, of necessity. For the Soviet government his company was erecting an automobile plant but had no concern in its future beyond training its men in the Ford plants, giving the use of blueprints and plans, and keeping the Russians informed of technical progress in America. All of this was being done at cost, and without a cent of interest in the investment.

The Ford rubber venture in Brazil was pushed forward in the belief that the use of rubber would increase so rapidly that soon no existing source of supply would be able to supply even a part of the demand. "The wise course," Ford said, "is not to monopolize present trade in rubber, but to prepare for the greatly increased demand." In the Brazilian operation, as in his other foreign enterprises, he made no effort to gain concessions and privileges or to slip into a preferred position, but went ahead on the same basis as other industries. He still had to face the old criticism of "American invasion," in contrast to the welcome given in this country to foreign industries which sought to do business here. Also he found foreigners complaining about "American standardization." As to that, as he has often said, he could only try to prove by his products what he could not prove by words, that his aim was to standardize the production of something to make life easier rather than to standardize life itself. Of the results of his expansion abroad he wrote:

Our company has had a measure of success in foreign business based on two principles: first, taking to the nations a commodity that they needed and the use of which assisted them to develop their own affairs, and second, an absolute renunciation of every form of exploitation. That is, our purpose was not to make American business greater at the expense of other nations, but to help make other peoples more prosperous by the aid of American business. There can be no other abiding basis for foreign business by any company or any country. And even then there will be no abiding relationship of seller and buyer between nations. International exchange of goods will always exist, of course, but not always of the same goods or in the same quantities. One great effect of American business abroad may be to teach our foreign customers how to supply themselves with the goods they now buy from us. Undoubtedly many countries now more or less dependent on industrial countries for supply will themselves become sufficiently industrial to supply their own requirements. That is, in commercial language, we will lose the market. But that is all to the good. As progressive beings we should look forward with approval to the time when new nations or backward nations shall outgrow their dependence and feel little or no further need for us. At that time international trade will then settle to the natural basis of need and supply, each nation supplying others with that commodity which it is most fitted to produce. This outlook is probably little relished by the heated salesmanship of the times, but it seems to be what is coming.

Russia came to us and asked assistance toward planting the automobile industry in that country, and although we shall have no authority or interest in the industry that will be established there, we readily consented on the principle that it is never wrong to help people to get to work and that the automobile is an instrument of social prosperity.

Our other activities outside the United States were formerly all operated under our sole ownership, but with the development of industrial effort abroad we have felt that our factories ought to belong in part to the people of the countries amongst whom we were doing business. After consideration of all that was involved, and feeling that if we know what is right to do nothing remains but to do it, we began the organization of our business abroad on a partnership basis, starting with the Ford Motor Company of England. I am glad to say that European industrialists have welcomed a complete demonstration of our principles in the various countries, and although it is not always at first clear to them how they can fully approve our rate of wages, yet there is no doubt in my mind that the desire to improve the lot of Europe's workingmen is so strong in progressive European industrialists that a way to better wages will be found. It is one thing to criticize the European industrialist and another thing to understand his problems, but I am sure that industrial leadership in Europe will bring about much social betterment there without mere imitation of American ways. They are too wise to be mere imitators of us, for then they would have to take our defects, too, which is not desirable.

On a site of 306 acres acquired in the previous year at Dagenham, eighteen miles from London, was started the construction of a central plant that would be the second largest in the world—next to River Rouge. Dagenham manufactures, assembles, distributes, and markets for Great Britain, Ireland, and some of the British possessions. With a frontage on the Thames, the plant has facilities for water, rail, and motor transport, and its principal fuel for producing 30,000 kilowatts of electric power is the London refuse which for hundreds of years was burned. In style the buildings are like those at River Rouge, but they were put up by British labor and with British materials, and all the machinery was built in England. The manufacturing and labor policies are the same as in the American factories.

Besides the manufacturing centers in America and England, the smaller Ford plants, some of them used for manufacturing and all of them for assembly and distribution, continued active through 1930 and into 1931, when the depression caused a slackening. To name only a few of the plants which served every quarter of the globe, these may be listed: Buenos Aires, Montevideo, Yokohama, São Paulo, Mexico City, and Santiago de Chile. The South American plants were linked directly with Dearborn and River Rouge, while in Germany, France, Holland, and Belgium the same policy was pursued as in Great Britain: the organization of separate companies, with part of their stock held by citizens of those countries.

Ford went ahead with the outside activities which had always interested him. Education of children and young men in the practical arts was one of them. He has characterized it as "education for leadership." The beneficiaries are residents of neighborhoods near his plants and experimental farms, largely the families of employees.

Headquarters of the system are the Edison Institute of Technology at Dearborn and the historic exhibit known as the Greenfield Village. The village and the Edison Museum adjoin, forming together the laboratory in which are demonstrated the inventions and appliances of centuries. To the institute come boys and young men from the scattered primary schools, examples of which are the schools at the Wayside Inn, South Sudbury, Mass., and at the Greenfield Village itself, where the small boys and girls have classes in the same red schoolhouse Ford attended as a boy. The Ford Trade School of the Highland Park and River Rouge plants is the best known link in the chain. Another, which has flourished since 1915, is the Apprentice School; when the problem of finding competent tool-makers became increasingly difficult, because the fashioning of precision tools and dies required more skill as mechanical knowledge advanced, this school was started with fifteen students; it has grown until as many as thirty-five hundred are to be seen in its classes at River Rouge.

Every pupil of the Ford schools, according to the theory of the system, is self-supporting from a scholarship at the start and helps at least in a measure to support the schools. All of them earn something each year. They learn self-reliance. The slowest of them acquire practical experience for making a living. The Ford plants and exhibitions are their textbooks in the main, though the study of subjects ordinarily taught up to the high-school grades is not neglected. Indeed, students at the Ford Trade School are thoroughly grounded in standard school subjects. However, it is in the shop and laboratory that they get the teaching most important to them.

Under experienced craftsmen the older boys learn,

for example, about electricity, machinery of every sort, the extraction of iron ore, the grinding of flour, and the making of an automobile from top to bottom. At the institute the ages range from seventeen to nineteen years, in the trade school from thirteen to eighteen. Courses are not fixed, nor methods stationary. The boy is taught to do what seems to suit his natural bent. Many graduate into jobs at the Ford plants; others go elsewhere, for no attempt is made to hold them longer than they want to stay, and the founder takes pride in scattering his alumni into different industries.

The boys of the trade school, after each week spent in classrooms on the usual elementary subjects, spend two weeks in the school shops working for the Ford Motor Company, which pays for their output at current rates and accepts nothing without a thorough inspection. The eight-hour day is established for pupils. The pay ranges from twenty cents an hour for sixteen-year-olds to thirty-five cents for students of eighteen years. Every six weeks a student's record is taken, and he gets an advance of one to three cents an hour, if his work has warranted it. The pupils do all the incidental work of caring for the school, performing janitor service, cooking and serving meals, and keeping the rooms painted and in good repair.

Pay as you go, with no stopping of your education for lack of funds; learn to fill any one of a thousand jobs, with skilled teachers at your elbow and a complete machine equipment at your command; study the subject that suits your temperament and ability, always in classes or workrooms scientifically ventilated and lighted—that is the scheme of the Ford schools.

The rest of the industrial world, like the Ford organization, had not begun to feel the full force of depression in 1930, nor to realize it was in for a long period of trouble.

A new German steamship, the *Europa*, made a new westward speed record across the Atlantic on her maiden voyage, crossing from Cherbourg to New York Harbor in four days, seventeen hours, and six minutes—a record soon to be bettered by her previously launched sister ship, the *Bremen*, with an eastward run of four days and fourteen hours. In fifteen years there had been as marked progress in ocean passenger carriers as in automobiles, and with the aid of the wireless and the lessons taught by the *Titanic* disaster it seemed that science had minimized marine perils. No major accidents interfered with the two and a quarter millions of Americans who traveled to foreign ports in the year. The size and luxury of ocean liners had increased until the regular Atlantic services included four steamships of more than fifty thousand tons, eight between forty and fifty thousand, and seven between thirty and forty thousand.

Peace movements occupied the statesmen's attention. The Senate ratified the London Naval Reduction Treaty, France completed the evacuation of the Ruhr, and as business conditions went from bad to worse there was much talk of peace conferences to come. But in 1931 Japan administered a blow to anti-militarist hopes by seizing large territories from China. The Smoot-Hawley Tariff Law of the previous year, meanwhile, had not been conducive to good feeling toward this country.

In a decade, as the census of 1930 showed, the population of the United States had grown from 105,710,-620 to 122,775,046.

Airplane feats continued through the two years in which business was sliding downward. Major Kingsford-Smith and three aides flew from Ireland to Newfoundland, then to Long Island and across to California, completing a round-the-world tour which had been begun in 1928; a British dirigible sailed to Montreal; four German aviators led by Capt. von Gronau voyaged from Sylt Island, in the North Sea, to the Faroe Islands, Iceland, Greenland, Labrador, Nova Scotia, and New York; Coste and Bellonte, making the first westward non-stop air journey to New York from the European continent, came from Paris in a few minutes over thirty-seven hours; the immense German seaplane *DO-X* crossed from the Cape Verde Islands to Brazil and up the coast to New York; Post and Gatty flew around the world, from Long Island and back again, a total of 15,474 miles, in less than nine days; Hillig and Hoiriis crossed from Newfoundland to Germany, and on the next day Magyar and Endress from Newfoundland to Hungary; Boardman and Polando broke transoceanic distance records, going from Brooklyn to Istanbul, Turkey; Herndon and Pangborn flew from Brooklyn to Wales, and on to Japan, whence, after they had been held on a charge of photographing forbidden areas, they crossed the Pacific to Wenatchee, Wash., and returned to Brooklyn; Colonel and Mrs. Lindbergh started on a round-the-world trip, reaching Alaska, Siberia, Japan, and China, passing over the Yangste River flood region, where 250,000 Chinese had been drowned, and returning home by steamship because of the sudden death of Mrs. Lindbergh's father, Senator Dwight W. Morrow; the *Graf Zeppelin* made the first of her South Atlantic return trips; Hinkler flew from Brazil to Senegal in West Africa. There had been a major casualty of the air in each year—the burning of the British dirigible *R-101* in France, with a loss of seventeen lives, and the disappearance of Parker D. Cramer and Oliver Parquette in the North Sea, after they had traveled safely from America to Hudson Bay, Baffin Land, Greenland, Iceland, and the Faroe and Shetland Islands.

The business of commercial aviation grew by leaps. Europe had passenger lines reaching all the principal cities, and regular travel by air was ceasing to be a novelty. The United States was not far behind. Mails were carried on schedule, and passenger lines were beginning to cover the map. Among the manufacturers was Ford, from whose plane factory at Dearborn emerged massive transports.

New concrete mileage in the United States reached its maximum of 9,935 miles constructed in 1930, not including city and town pavings, and did not fall off until two years later. The surfaced highways of the country were now 730,000 miles out of a total of more than 3,000,000 miles of roads; the taxes for highways had reached a billion and a half dollars a year, and the sum spent on the nation's roads was slightly in excess of that. There were more than 25,000,000 motor vehicles in the country, nearly 20 per cent of them trucks. At the same time (1930) farm tractors numbered 920,000, telephones on farms more than 2,000,-000, and radios on farms far over 1,000,000. State gasoline taxes exceeded $500,000,000. Ninety-nine thousand buses were in operation on our roads.

Toward the end of 1930 it became evident, except to the most optimistic or the least informed, that depressed business conditions had come to stay a while. A conspicuous episode in the wake of the speculative craze was the collapse of the Bank of the United States, in New York City, as a result of which depositors and stockholders lost millions. Unemployment increased alarmingly. The government became a machine for devising preventive measures to ward off further trouble, and the good or bad results of such devices are still a topic of discussion.

From the beginning of bad times Henry Ford dissented from the theory that prices should be forced up and wages generally cut, and that output should be curtailed by agreement or law. He repeated his belief that a company which failed to meet market conditions, good or bad, had itself to blame. Bad management, not outside forces, was the cause of business decline, he insisted, and there was something the matter with an industry's service and leadership if it collapsed. He blamed the speculative mania for the industrial troubles, for the stoppage of improvement in manufactured goods and the failure to improve manufacturing methods. Proper leadership, he argued, would effect economies in order to lower prices, instead of raising them.

"There has been no overproduction of quality goods, for which a market still exists and always will exist," he declared. "Never had there been overproduction in the true sense that it resulted in no market for needed goods at the lowest possible prices."

That continued to be his viewpoint as the depression progressed. How rapidly it progressed, here and in other countries, is recalled by a few outstanding incidents: Popular unrest caused the overthrow of governments in Bolivia, Peru, Argentina, and Brazil in 1930, and of Spain, Peru (a second time), Chile, Paraguay, and Salvador in 1931. On June 20, 1931, President Hoover proposed the moratorium on intergovernmental debts, after conditions in Germany had become so demoralized that they threatened the world's financial systems. This was the White House's first open avowal indicating that the situation was getting out of hand.

In the following August the Labor Ministry resigned in England, but Ramsay MacDonald kept the helm of the new régime backed by a union of the older parties, which overwhelmed the laborites at the polls. In September Great Britain suspended the gold standard, an example soon followed by the nations dependent on London for their financial policies. The Premier of France journeyed to Washington to confer with President Hoover in October, and a month later came the Italian Foreign Minister.

As the year drew to a close, the Ford Motor Company was naturally feeling the pressure, and Henry Ford was already making preparations for another new car —a "universal car" again—that would be able to weather bad times as long as they might last and to ride the tide into the new good times which were sure to come. However, the year which brought disaster to many businesses had seen his company still moving forward, with five new assembly plants built, production started by the English at Dagenham, and the twenty-millionth Ford automobile turned out of the River Rouge factory.

This twenty-millionth car—Model A improved by four years of technical changes, more spacious, with a longer wheelbase, a lower hung chassis, and a heavier frame—made a tour of the United States and was greeted with noisy celebrations everywhere. Though the public was not aware of it, Ford had been experimenting more than a year on an eight-cylinder engine at his Dearborn laboratory. In fact, he had been thinking about an eight-cylinder motor for reasonably priced cars as far back as 1921. The time was not yet ripe for its appearance, he decided, so he put the latest four-cylinder into production for the 1932 trade. Not even his closest associates expected the sudden change of plan which was to be ordered a few months afterward.

VII
A "UNIVERSAL CAR" AGAIN: THE V-8

At the beginning of 1932 the world had accommodated itself to motor traffic on nearly nine million miles of highways, of which more than two fifths were in the United States and Canada. Unrest and unemployment were having less effect on motor-making and road-building than on other industries, though they also were suffering. Political disturbances and a prevalence of nostrums for remedying business were evident everywhere.

Henry Ford, although he had spent a long time experimenting with the eight-cylinder engine and in making up his mind when to produce it, acted quickly when he reached a decision. He gave notice in February that he intended to offer an eight but would continue to manufacture the four-cylinder Model A. In March he appeared at his laboratory one morning, spent a few hours with his principal aides from River Rouge, and ordered them to stop production in the plants immediately. His men were taken completely by surprise, as was the public when an announcement was made of the sudden move. Only Ford himself was not excited. The hundred millions of dollars he had spent recasting his plants and machinery in preparation for Model A were to be regarded only as an investment in experience, along with current deficits in a falling market and the huge outlay about to be undertaken in launching the eight-cylinder car. It was no time for wistful waiting. Ford did not like a falling market, and something had to be done about it.

"Yes, we are going to keep prices down so that the public can buy our cars," was his complacent answer to a newspaper man's question, at a time when the business community's chorus was a lament over the people's lost buying power. "We shall continue to make the four-cylinder model. The eight is only two fours, you know."

While plant reorganization for the added product was costly, the change did not begin to compare with that of 1927. Only sections of factories, not whole plants, had to be left idle during new installations of machinery. The eight-cylinder car, known as the V-8, was introduced gradually, beginning within a month.

On the principle that a fine appearance and a maximum of comfort had come to be necessities rather than luxuries in automobiles, the V-8 was the handsomest of Ford creations. For the first time a V-type of engine, with 65 horsepower, was put in a low-priced car; but, like all Ford engines, it was simple in design, each of the two four-cylinder banks being cast in a single piece with the crankcase. An automatic spark, synchronized gear shifting, rubber mountings at scores of points to lessen noise, a double-drop frame, and rustless steel were among the features of the car, which was advertised as the last word in economical maintenance. And it was capable of great speed. Both the eight and the four continued in quantity production through the year. Each was offered in fourteen body styles. Their appearance on the market, incidentally, followed close on the heels of two new types of the Lincoln, the company's more expensive product, whose engines were now built with eight or twelve cylinders.

When the V-8 was put on display, March 31st, between five and six million people visited the Ford showrooms, and on April 9th the Governor of Michigan attended a celebration, with a banquet and ball, at Dearborn. The prices ranged from $460 to $650 for the V-8, and from $410 to $600 for the Model A. Other achievements of the year included the opening of new assembly plants at Seattle, Mexico City, and Amsterdam, Holland, and service branches at Alexandria, Va., and Lisbon, Portugal.

So the latest "universal car" got started on its career, in spite of general business conditions that went from bad to worse, although the statistics showed that thirty-three and a half million motor vehicles were now registered in the world, two thirds of them in this country.

In that year of 1932 the world went through some novel and unpleasant experiences. The Brazilian government burned or sank in the ocean millions of bags of coffee in an effort to lift prices. Groups of unemployed marched to Washington. Italy ordered the death penalty for violators of emergency laws. The two-billion-dollar Reconstruction Finance Corporation bill was passed by Congress and signed by President Hoover. Cabinet after cabinet rose and fell in France. Continued revolutionary outbreaks and strikes kept Spain in a state bordering on anarchy, and the new republican rulers confiscated all Church property. Reparation conferences dragged on, without the payment of war debts. The Japanese invaded Shanghai, alleging a Chinese boycott of Japanese goods, and defied the League of Nations, from which they subsequently withdrew. The first World Conference on Disarmament opened at Genoa.

No sensation of our day has equaled the kidnaping of the Lindbergh baby, on March 1st. Kidnapings increased, and the other numerous "rackets" of the underworld prospered.

The United States Senate voted a stock exchange inquiry which was to last beyond the Hoover Administration. Henry Pu Yi, former Chinese Emperor, was installed as "dictator" of the new state of Manchukuo, while the Japanese continued to run its affairs. Ivar Kreuger, his chain of trusts on the verge of collapse, committed suicide. Hindenburg was reëlected President of the German Reich, defeating Hitler. J. P. Morgan made a radio speech, urging support for the block plan to relieve the unemployed. President Hoover repeated his demands for governmental economies. Great Britain doubled her general 10 per cent tariff. Civil war ravaged China, which was helpless against continued invasions by Japan. Paul Doumer, the new President of France, was assassinated, and Albert Lebrun was elected to succeed him. President Hoover, insisting that Congress balance the budget, issued a public attack on the lobbyists swarming over Washington.

Amelia Earhart Putnam, flying alone, took her plane from Newfoundland to Ireland, and other daring flights followed. Colonel von Papen succeeded Bruening as German Chancellor. John D. Rockefeller, Jr., hitherto a supporter of National Prohibition, announced that he had decided it was a failure. The "bonus army" camped in Washington. The United States government reported a financial deficit of nearly three billion dollars at the close of the fiscal year in June. Congress, before adjourning in July, adopted the two-billion-dollar unemployment relief bill and a system of home loan discount banks. The St. Lawrence Waterway Treaty was signed by the United States and Canada. Mayor "Jimmy" Walker of New York resigned while under charges. A second son was born to the Lindberghs. Farmers went on strike in the Middle West, preventing delivery of foodstuffs. Two hundred thousand cotton operatives struck in England. "Hunger marchers" rioted in London, and many were injured by police clubs.

War in the Chaco region between Bolivia and Peru grew into a relentless struggle, destined to continue for years. President Hoover notified European nations that the United States could not agree to a postponement of their debt payments. Another Cabinet overturn in Germany resulted in the brief Chancellorship of General von Schleicher. France defaulted on her debt payment to the United States, and Premier Herriot resigned; other defaulters were Belgium, Hungary, Poland, and Esthonia, while payments were made by Great Britain, Italy, Czechoslovakia, Finland, Lithuania, and Latvia.

The Presidential campaign, the bitterest in a generation, did nothing to contribute toward restoring calm at home or abroad. For the greater part of the year, starting with the preliminary skirmishes before the party conventions and ending on Election Day in November, it added recurrent irritation to the uncertainty of industry, employers and employed alike.

After President Hoover announced his candidacy for reëlection, his renomination by the Republicans was assured, despite grumblings in the party. The Democratic camp, on the contrary, remained in a turmoil until the convention named Franklin D. Roosevelt, with John N. Garner as his running mate. There was never any serious doubt of a Democratic victory. The voters of the country were determined on a change of administration, and Mr. Roosevelt soon had their confidence.

The contest developed differences of opinion over policies toward business and over the liquor question, with Roosevelt for outright prohibition repeal and Hoover favoring action by the different states to suit themselves. Roosevelt announced that he was for a "New Deal," the rescue of the "Forgotten Man," and "social justice through social action." He accused the opposition of spreading "the gospel of fear" and said he was fighting "the four horsemen of distress, delay, deceit, and despair." Hoover, as the grueling controversy drew to a close, said that if the Democratic tariff were put into effect the grass would grow "in the streets of a hundred cities." The election betting was seven to one against the Republicans, and on November 4th the vote for Roosevelt exceeded 22,000,000, while Hoover's was below 16,000,000.

From Election Day until the inauguration in the following March, efforts were made by Hoover to form an alliance with Roosevelt for the solution of pending difficulties. They had meetings in the White House at the President's invitation, but the President-elect thought it wise to assume no responsibility for shaping new policies or amending old ones until his installation as Chief Executive.

Meanwhile, business lagged, and the country waited. There were, of course, exceptional cases of industrial leaders who devoted their energies to combating the prevailing pessimism with constructive activities. One of them was Ford. He pushed his new car with all the ingenuity he possessed and said little. What he did say was by way of repetition of his old belief that the public would always find a way of buying what it needed, if the price was right.

The stamina of the V-8 was put to the test on a 10,000-mile run by Eddie Pullen, a professional driver. He traveled at the rate of 1,000 miles a day, averaging 48 miles an hour for the whole distance, making 18.35 miles to the gallon of gasoline, using only one and a half pints of oil each day, and adding only five and one half quarts of water to the radiator during the whole ten-days' run. Gross sales for the year were nearly $259,-000,000. But they had exceeded $462,000,000 in 1931, and $873,000,000 in 1930, and in 1929 they had risen above $1,000,000,000.

The annual round-up of figures for the motor industry in 1932 showed, among a hundred other details, that the number of buses in the country had increased to 105,000, that 96 per cent of passenger cars were of the closed type, and that 62 per cent of automobiles were purchased by persons with incomes below $3,000 a year.

An improved V-8, the second of its family, was brought out at the beginning of 1933. With a 75 horse-power engine, it could run 84 miles an hour. Again there were fourteen different styles. The car had a longer wheelbase. Its body, all steel, was roomier. Stress was laid upon the aluminum cylinder heads and the X-type frame. Safety glass was in all windshields, and the de luxe models were equipped with it throughout, besides having cowl lights, two tail lights, and two horns. Ford, having gone in for decorative finish, was not forgetting any of the fine touches. The price range was $475 to $610. At the same time the new V-8 trucks were put on sale, from $320 to $500.

We have never yet had a sufficient production of all the things which the family needs [ran a public statement over Ford's signature]. It would be splendid if the world should seriously attempt to overproduce everything that every-body needs. We should then discover that our present ma-chine facilities could not even catch up with the need. Give the world a money system that makes it easier for goods to flow from man to man, and all the factories on earth could not begin to supply a tenth of the demand.

Always adept at short phrases in appealing to his market, he said:

We do not build a low-price car. The cost to us of build-ing our car is pretty expensive. But we do build a high-quality car at a low price.

Also he was now turning out his higher priced car, the Lincoln, with different wheelbases, 136 and 145 inches; but, as he had often said, this automobile was not designed for a commodity. His salesmanship talents were still devoted to the "universal car."

In a series of signed advertisements he rang the changes on the economic operation of the V-8, "the only eight-cylinder car at a low price with the qualification of the high-priced eight-cylinder cars." A Ford entry in a California race made an official record of 79.21 miles an hour for 235 miles. Before the year's end twenty-six of the thirty-two assembly plants in the United States had closed, as well as the blast furnaces, steel mills, and glass plant, and production was reduced to the rate of 400,000 cars a year. The capacity of the vast system of plants was still two million cars a year. Ford concluded that it might be unwise for an organization to thresh itself to tatters in an attempt to stimulate business. He turned to the task of consolidating his organization and further improving his product, in preparation for the time when the business situation should improve. "No use being all worn out when the tide turns," he said. "Take it easy and get ready."

It was at this stage that the great furore arose over N. R. A., as the department administering the National Industrial Recovery Act came to be called. But much had happened before attention centered on that most controversial phase of the New Deal.

The immediate result of Roosevelt's inaugural address, with its keynote of "action, and action now," was an extraordinary burst of optimism throughout the country. The change of administrations had a profound effect on the mental state of the people. Pessimism had pervaded all parts of the country, with the

banks closed in most states and business almost at a
standstill, but that President Roosevelt immediately
won tremendous popularity was not gainsaid anywhere.

As in all national crises, the excitement over a new
order subsided by degrees, and the country settled down

LUNCH HOUR AT FORD HEADQUARTERS
*The inventor, with his son and chief aides, at a regular daily
meeting.*

to working and watching. Spirited action, meanwhile,
began at Washington immediately after the inauguration, with the closing of all banks and stock exchanges,
accompanied by the gold embargo and the requisition-
ing of private gold holdings. Without delay Congress,
with few dissenting voices, adopted a series of measures
giving the President temporary dictatorial power over

finance and business and authorizing him to cut half a billion dollars from federal expenses. The Senate and House quickly acceded to his request for the legalization of beer sales. In less than a fortnight 13,541 of the 17,600 banks in the country were open again, "conservators" were in charge of many depositories to get their affairs in shape, and recovery seemed surely under way.

Legislative and executive orders in pursuance of the "New Deal" followed one another daily, and on several occasions the President talked informally over the radio, telling the citizenry what he was doing. The reforestation plan was established to give work to a quarter of a million men. The farm relief and the half-billion-dollar unemployment relief bills were passed without much opposition. The government took control of Muscle Shoals. Investigation of stock exchanges was continued by the Senate and resulted in the passage of the control bill.

The National Industrial Recovery Act was passed by Congress just before it adjourned for the summer. General Hugh S. Johnson was appointed administrator over the country's industries under the recovery law, and a new word—or an old word with a new meaning —entered the American vocabulary. Code! For each industry a code was prescribed. The codification began with the larger manufacturing and production lines, such as motorcars, steel, oil, textiles, lumber, building, and railroads, but extended all the way down to the smallest groups. Less than a year after General Johnson took hold, Washington reported 400 codes signed, and the pending hearings on regularity agreements were attended by a variety of business specialists, in-

cluding the Corset and Brassière Manufacturers, the
Men's Garter Makers, and representatives of two hundred other lines.

Along with N. R. A. were brought into being a score
or more other major bureaus, each of which came to
be known by its initials. The Agricultural Adjustment
Administration, designed to improve the farmers' condition, ranked next to N. R. A. in cost and scope.

President Roosevelt signed the Cotton Textile Code
on July 9th, abolishing child labor and fixing minimum
wages. Critics of N. R. A. contended in the main that
the government was overstepping its function in interfering with private business and initiative, that regi-
mentation of American industry was contrary to the
law and spirit of the country, and that the small
business man in particular was being imposed upon by
a system in which he had no chance to combat the
competition of corporate wealth. The President had
said at the start of his administration that he expected
to make mistakes and would not hesitate to rectify
them. Drastic revisions of the act in 1934 were doubtless in pursuance of this reassuring statement.

At the height of the mass enthusiasm for N. R. A.
the automobile industry, after much discussion, signed
a code, and the country was startled to discover that
Henry Ford was not among the signers. No official
statement has ever come from Ford or the Ford Motor
Company as to the reason for this attitude. It is,
however, sufficiently known that Ford's decision was
not without the weightiest reasons. It may be said that
he reached his decision alone. Those who believed that
he was right had little confidence that it could be made

to appear to the American buying public that he was right. Ford's refusal to oppose the President by explaining his own position added to that fear. It was as if Ford had said to himself, "The President must do what he thinks is right without hindrance, and I can only do what I think is right." Talk of "boycott" and "cracking down" was rife in the country, and well organized attempts were made to make it seem unpatriotic to buy a Ford car. The unexpected result was that in a few weeks the sale of Ford cars increased to greater volume than for several years previous.

Ford's attitude rested on what he considered sound basis in reason and fact. He believed that the suspension of anti-trust laws and the suppression of honest competition was un-American and basically injurious to American progress. He believed that N. R. A. was unconstitutional, but he was not at all concerned to test it in the courts—the President must be left free to work his own plans as far as they could be made to work. But Ford the engineer knew that nothing can be made to work by decree; it must be of right design. He believed, moreover, that the law as laid down by the government must be obeyed by every citizen, and it was admitted on all sides that not only did Ford comply with N. R. A. requirements, but exceeded them in all particulars. He had been exceeding them for years. A saying attributed to him at the time was, "If I lived up to N. R. A., I would have to live down to it." As a matter of fact, many N. R. A. requirements had been inaugurated by Ford fifteen years before. And lastly he believed that signing a code was no part of the law, and that in refusing to sign a code he was not resisting the law nor obstructing the recovery program. In June, 1934, the government itself conceded this point by announcing that all non-signers of codes who were complying with the law were entitled to fly the Blue Eagle. At the same time, however, an executive order which made it impossible for any Ford dealer to sell cars to the government remained, rather illogically, in effect. That this, with other disabilities, have since been removed, testifies to the essential soundness of Ford's position in the first place.

The justice and American character of Ford's stand soon became apparent to the nation at large, and threats of "boycott" and "cracking down" ceased to be heard. It was a tribute to a man who did his own thinking and was willing to take heavy losses rather than compromise on principle. His absolute silence on the question, his refusal of every offer of the widest publicity for any word of self-defense he might consent to utter at the most critical hour of concentrated opposition to him, was based on his confidence in the ability of the people to reach a correct understanding of his position. This and his refusal by any word of his to oppose the President's program, constitute the entire available explanation of one of the most daring instances of individual action in recent American history. To this, of course, must be added Henry Ford's thirty years' insistence on social justice and the New Deal for American workingmen, all of which have been part of his personal management of the Ford Motor Company.

Among the important happenings of 1933—outside of the United States government's activities, which dwarfed all other news—were the continued moves of Japan for extension of their domain into Chinese areas, the death of ex-President Coolidge, riots in Spain, the institution of long-distance electric train service on the Pennsylvania Railroad from New York to Philadelphia, ratification of the "Lame Duck" Constitutional amendment providing that Congress would hereafter hold a single regular annual session beginning in January, the election of De Valera as President of the Irish Free State, Hitler's accession to the chancellorship and practical dictatorship of Germany, the attempt of an assassin on President-elect Roosevelt shortly before his inauguration, Congress's vote to submit the prohibition question to State conventions and ratification of the repeal amendment within less than a year, the wreck of the United States Navy dirigible *Akron* with a loss of seventy-two lives, "token payments" on the June installments of war debts by several nations, and full payment by Finland alone, unproductive sessions of the World Disarmament Conference at Geneva, the meeting of the World Economic Conference in London, periodic labor strikes, the naval building program to cost $130,000,000, the Cuban revolution, Germany's withdrawal from the League of Nations and Disarmament Conference, New York City's departure from her custom of electing a Tammany mayor, and the United States' recognition of the Russian Soviet Union.

Aviation records had ceased to be novelties in 1933, but the flyers continued their adventures. Wiley Post, traveling alone, flew the 15,596 miles of the Northern route around the world in less than eight days. Colonel and Mrs. Lindbergh made the circle, stopping in many lands and studying routes from the viewpoint of practical transport service. James Mattern's journey around the earth was completed after accidents and delays.

Ocean crossings included that of General Italo Balbo, Italian War Minister, and his fleet of fourteen seaplanes, which visited the Chicago Exposition and returned home by way of the Azores; a record non-stop flight from New York to Syria, 5,653 miles, by Rossi and Codos, the same Frenchmen who in 1934 were to

A Ford tri-motor plane.

make the second successful flight westward from the Continent to New York; trips over the South Atlantic by two planes, piloted by Mermoz, a Frenchman, and Skarzinski, a Pole; the flight of James A. Mollinson and his wife (Amy Johnson) from Wales to Connecticut, ending in a forced landing at Bridgeport, and the ill-fated venture of Barbera and Collar, Spanish army officers, who flew to Cuba and then disappeared on the way to Mexico. British aviators took two planes over Mount Everest. The world's air speed record of 423.7 miles an hour was made by Francesco Agello, an Italian warrant officer.

Ford had slowed down in manufacturing airplanes. Although Ford ships have flown 1,500,000 miles in Ford service, and over 24,000,000 miles in the service of the various airlines, and though at the end of the year air transport lines stretched over 26,221 miles in this country and 19,875 miles abroad, Ford had ideas concerning progress in aviation which had never been satisfied. His suspension of active interest is probably temporary; his associates say he will go into aircraft production again if he can produce something that he considers an advance step in aviation. Meanwhile his airport makes repairs of ships in service, for which he keeps his shops ready at all times. Ford ships rank high in safety and reliability, though recently they have been exceeded as to speed.

With the new year of 1934, the industries of the country, while showing a measurable improvement, were not all making enough gains to boast about. There were still dark spots on the prosperity map. However, unemployment had decreased, profits were again the order in many factories, and prospects were rosier nearly everywhere. At the close of 1933 the Ford production had shown a slow increase, with the gross sales for the year somewhat better.

Of a sudden, the whole picture changed at Dearborn in the first month of 1934. The millions and the thought it had cost to get through the past two years were forgotten in the enthusiasm of Ford's department heads over the increased output in January—57,575 cars, or 25 per cent more than had been planned when the year opened. It was the greatest monthly output since June, 1932. Forty-one million dollars went for wages and materials, an increase of 50 per cent in wages and 300 per cent in materials over the previous January. The assembly plants in Norfolk, Va., and Dallas, Tex., were reopened, and others got into action soon afterward. Nearly two years had been needed to establish the V-8, but apparently it had now "arrived."

Having introduced his third eight-cylinder model in December, Ford soon let the country know what the "universal car" of 1934 was like. Along with much printed advertising, he started his first radio broadcast, which, as Edsel Ford announced in a talk at the microphone, was intended to be an agreeable concert for the air audience and not a mere excuse for intrusive speeches on the Ford product.

The new car was the only one with a V-type engine and eight cylinders selling below $2,000. While prices were raised $5.00 to $35, owing to increased costs, the roadster was offered for $525 and the most expensive of the eleven styles, the victoria, at $610. This de luxe vehicle had two unique new features, a divided three-passenger front seat and a large luggage compartment in the rear. There were other types no less luxurious. All the models had the dual carburetor and dual intake, the X-frame, the longer wheelbase, and the aluminum cylinder heads. Betterments in engine details had increased the speed, acceleration, and mileage capacity, which was twenty miles to a gallon at a forty-five-mile speed. Thermostats in the water lines enabled the engine to heat up more quickly and to maintain the right temperature. Oil consumption was reduced. The ventilating system was designed to let in air without drafts.

By the end of February sales in Wayne County, which includes Detroit, were three times those of any other car in the low-price field. In the Gilmore race for stock cars at Los Angeles, twenty-two of the twenty-six entrants drove Fords, and ten of them took the first ten places, the winner averaging 62.367 miles an hour over a track that was nearly all curves. Previously on a straighter course a V-8 had averaged 80.22 miles an hour.

All this was big news at River Rouge and the other Ford plants. The newspaper columns at the time were filled with echoes of the Presidential order canceling air-mail contracts, the multitude of investigations in progress or proposed, rumors of wars, scandals of politics, the ramifications of N. R. A., and other matters remote from southern Michigan. But politics, government policies, the record-breaking February snowfalls, and the news of the world in general were of small concern at River Rouge by comparison with the charts which showed production rising up and up.

Ford made another quick decision that month—to put on a great show at the Century of Progress Exposition in Chicago. The fair, having closed one successful run, was scheduled to open again in May, and it was no simple matter to prepare an exhibit costing $2,000,-000 in so short a time. Not a piece of the steel frame was on the site by the end of the month, but in less than sixty days the framework of the Ford building was finished. The structure was a sixth of a mile long, on an eleven-acre plot facing Lake Michigan. Into its halls and galleries were brought the inventor's treasured museum pieces showing transportation development through the centuries. On the grounds was laid out an oval track paved in sections to reproduce bits of road representative of the ages, from Roman cobblestones down to the concrete of today. Ample space was left for a miniature experimental soy bean farm, a promenade along the waterfront, graceful terraces, and an outdoor concert enclosure in which to seat a large orchestra and audience.

The Chicago exhibit plan was a multiple of the show idea which had been used in a smaller way at various places. In the Seattle assembly plant, for example, a recent exhibition had included a Russian droshky four hundred years old, a London cab, a Paris landau, and an Oriental rickshaw. At Dearborn the permanent museum of the Edison Institute had been growing for years, and from there came the antiques and machines for the Exposition building. In the operating departments of the exhibit at the Century of Progress, all displays exemplify the idea that the materials which form the automobile come from the earth and are fabricated by the ingenuity of man into a vehicle that carries him over the surface of the earth. Many of the exhibits start with the basic iron, cotton and copper in their raw form and show the actual methods by which the raw material is wrought into the finished part.

On March 13, 1934, after having made scattered increases of wages in the last year, Ford announced a restoration of the minimum basic daily rate of $5.00, affecting 47,000 of the 70,000 workers then in his plants. It was the first blanket raise since December, 1929, when the minimum went from $6.00 to $7.00. In disclosing his move, he warned workingmen against flocking to River Rouge.

"This is not a call for workers," he said. "Plenty of Detroit automobile employees are still out of work. We must take care of them first." He had been obliged to make a reduction of wages in 1931. "That was the hardest thing I ever had to do," he remarked.

For a few days he was besieged by interviewers. How was it possible, asked one of them, to keep his car prices down while labor and materials were going up? His reply was the old one: "When prices go up, business goes down." Higher wages were not an additional cost under proper management, he explained, for the better paid workman was more willing and efficient. As to the cost of materials—well, if the producers from whom he bought goods charged too much for them, he would make them for himself, as he had done before! Meanwhile, employment figures were rising, until in May the average number of workers at River Rouge was 48,000 a day, and in the domestic branches 25,000 a day.

The River Rouge Plant, which is three miles from Ford's headquarters in the laboratory at Dearborn and within sight of the road into Detroit, was again its old self in the spring of 1934. Production there and in the ten other plants now in operation was at the rate of 90,000 cars a month in May, or more than 1,000,000 a year. A constant procession of sightseers, of whom 185,000 pour into the gates and are guided through the

Open-hearth furnaces at River Rouge.

maze annually, witnessed a scene of bewildering activity
and went away dazed by the effort of trying to com-
prehend the interwoven activities of blast furnaces,
open-hearth furnaces, coke ovens, assembly lines, testing shops, the rolling mill, the foundry, miles of railway
tracks, and waterfront docks lined with steamships,
tugs, and all the paraphernalia of handling millions of
tons of ore and coal and other materials shipped into
the place in a twelvemonth.

Interspersed among the buildings, some of them long
low structures, others rising high into the air with still
higher smokestacks, the visitors saw plots of grass as
smooth as Ford's own lawn in Dearborn, while over the

network of concrete roads constant lines of motor trucks passed, supplementing the railway cars and steamships in moving freight to and from the plant. To tour the two square miles on foot would require many days. Moving rapidly in one of the company's service cars, a personally conducted guest is enabled to glimpse the high spots with the aid of inclined roadways, on which the car darts up to second-floor levels, along avenues of giant machinery, and out again to the ground. This system of ramps was constructed just before President Hoover went to Dearborn for the Edison Jubilee in 1929, but he lingered so long in Ford's historic village that he had no time to visit the plant.

The favored visitor must walk when he inspects the

Blast furnaces in the world's largest automobile plant.

foundry, where he wonders at the perfection of cleanliness and order amid so much noise of machinery and such a horde of workers. Not a murky windowpane, not a heap of litter is to be seen. The guide explains things as they pass through, but the scene changes so fast that one remembers only a succession of machines and artisans. The casting of the V-8 cylinder block in one piece, an achievement unknown until Ford contrived it, stands out among a welter of unaccustomed impressions.

Eventually the sightseer's path leads past the assembly lines, more than twenty-five miles of them. They move with never a pause, each conveyor at the proper speed for the adjustment of the part it is bearing toward the final assembly. Passing from the foundry to the machine shop, one watches the cylinder blocks grabbed by monster machines that drill eighty-six holes into them in one operation, and marvels at a hundred other operations performed on schedule to the split second. Finally, in the main assembly line, which is nearly a thousand feet long, the complete car is put together; having started as a bare frame, it collects its parts as it moves along. The radiator is lifted on and fastened down, the engine bolted into place, the wheels attached. The onlooker becomes so absorbed in watching one operation that the next one takes place before he can see it. At last he stops to look at what seems to the uninitiated the most striking incident of the tour—the fitting of a completed car body on the chassis.

Through an aperture overhead appears the body, hanging on a big hook at the end of a chain. It is painted and upholstered. Probably it has come from the

Briggs or the Murray works, which make most Ford bodies. It is one of a line that has been moving with unbroken precision up an incline, from a point several hundred feet away, to its position over the assembly line. After it is hitched to the chain, it descends with ponderous deliberation to meet the oncoming chassis. Workmen on each side push it gently into place as it swings in air. With a slight thud it settles on the frame. Men with tools poised are ready to bolt it on tight. Slowly then the car moves forward, while another body descends from above to meet another chassis.

About a minute after this procedure, a finished V-8 moves off the line under its own power and goes on its way—maybe to Detroit, or into one of the new leviathan trucks which take the cars assembled at River Rouge to cities within a radius of several hundred miles, as well as carrying parts to assembly branches within that range. The installation of the truck transport service is one of the new developments of the past year, and it has supplanted short-distance hauling by railway so far as Ford is concerned.

Another new activity is the reconditioning of used motors, at a cost of less than fifty dollars each. Arriving at the factory, the old engines traverse a "disassembly" line of their own, on which the process of taking them to pieces is exactly the reverse of the upbuilding process in the motor assembly line. Up to March, 1934, the reconditioning department had handled nearly thirty-nine thousand V-8 engines and more than one hundred and thirty-five thousand Model A motors.

What is known at River Rouge as the "reincarnation department" is a third novelty. It occurred to Ford that

Truck transports for cars and materials.

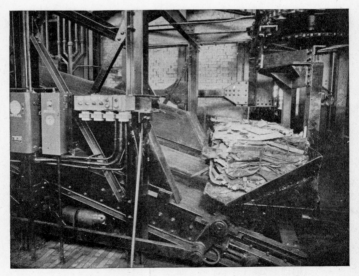

Junked cars and the "Reincarnation Department."

a vast quantity of waste resulted from junked cars, cast aside after they were beyond repairing. By finding a use for them, he could accomplish three things worth while —he could get them out of the automobile junk yards that had been unsightly spots near cities and towns, he could pay the owners a little money for something which was otherwise worth nothing, and he could furnish employment to a considerable number of workmen. A wreck is stripped until only its steel is left, and then, after being compressed in the largest bailing machines ever built, it is charged into an open-hearth furnace. One of the sights of a ride through the open-hearth building is the reincarnation of a junked car. Out of the furnaces, the glare from which is so dazzling that one look at it brings tears to the eyes, pours molten steel which is cast into cigar-shaped ingots a dozen feet long—all that remains of the once proud lord of the roads. Traveling through one press after another, on a trip perhaps a fifth of a mile long, the ingots are mashed into strips that look like railroad rails, and from them are fashioned various small parts for use in new cars. The expense of all this yields no saving as compared with making the parts from new metal. The "reincarnation department" is not a profit maker, but it pays its way.

On the trip through the River Rouge plant and experimental laboratories, one sees so much that it is impossible to remember a tithe of the lesson. He wishes he could understand it all—the measuring gauges, for example, which make it possible to fit together bits of metal with an accuracy of one millionth of an inch; the implements used in the testing rooms, which are surrounded by glass, and the thousand and one achievements of the foundry, machine shop, and assembly lines. As he drives away, his attention is diverted from the intricacies of these meticulous operations by the sight of a monster steel claw, which swings from a derrick beside two towering blast furnaces. The claw is like a monstrous hand. Reaching down into the hold of a steamship anchored alongside, it hoists an eleven-ton handful of ore, which has just arrived from the Superior region to be used with limestone and coke in the making of pig iron. The steamship, the guide remarks, is one of those put into service in 1934 after lying up for two years. At the Ford factories, as elsewhere, many things which were recently out of service are laid up no longer.

Before leaving the plant, the visitor may have been fortunate enough to meet the key men of the Administration Office Building, Edsel Ford, Sorensen, Martin, and the others. McCarroll, the chief chemist and metallurgist—though he has no such formal title—may have explained, if he could be persuaded to spare ten minutes, some of the scientific advances made in the past year, including the three new steel alloys one of which is being used to make the lighter and stronger crankshafts, turned out at the rate of 6,000 a day. He may have explained, too, the genesis of the latest valve push-rod, reduced in weight by one seventh of an ounce, and of a new wear-resisting material which reduces noise and makes it less necessary than ever before to have service on valves and push-rods. A year or so ago the metallurgist thought the valve push-rod could not be made lighter, but Ford

The new V-8.

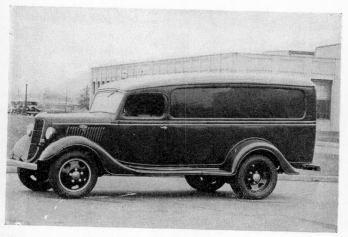

An eight-cylinder Ford truck.

walked in one day and insisted that it must be done. Months of experiments were necessary to get rid of that seventh of an ounce.

Another achievement of which one learns in the chemistry division is the new enamel paint used on Ford cars. It is manufactured from the oil of the soy bean, and for the 1934 models its durability has been so improved that only water is recommended as a polish. The testers at River Rouge have subjected shiny cars to all sorts of maltreatment in proving the toughness and durability of this enamel. You can freeze it, bake it, or expose it to the rays of the tropical sun for months without damaging its original lustre.

The soy bean furnishes a key exhibit for Ford's theory of the relation between agriculture and industry. Farmers, he says, have a bigger job than raising food alone. The soy bean is demonstrating that they can produce materials needed by industry, which eventually should be able to get its raw supplies without denuding forests for wood and without mining for ores.

Oil from soy beans is used by Ford for the lubricating of machinery as well as for making paint. From the pulpy residue of the beans he has already put into production various small parts of automobiles, including the horn button, light switch assembly, and the gearshift knob. The substance is being used to perfect a steering wheel, soon to be produced in quantities, replacing the wheel made of bakelite composition. It is estimated that a half bushel of the beans are now used in the construction of every Ford car. Even an imitation of steel has been fashioned out of them, and slabs of it are to be seen in Ford's laboratory. The synthetic metal appears to be as tough as steel. It is now going through innumerable experiments, with the view of using it to make entire car bodies. The use of beans in automobile manufacture seems to be only in its beginnings.

"How did he hit upon the soy bean?" one of Ford's chief assistants was asked.

"Soy beans were selected to illustrate the possible linking of farming and industry," was the answer, "because they are easier to grow in more widely varying localities, and rebuild rather than deplete the soil."

There are three thousand kinds of soy beans. Ford's experiments to identify the best variety are reminiscent of Edison's worldwide search for the most serviceable bamboo to use for a filament in the incandescent bulb. Out of twelve thousand acres under cultivation on the experimental farms in 1932, two thirds were devoted to beans. In 1933 the harvest was 100,000 bushels. There was no trouble finding uses for them. Not only are they becoming a standard source of automobile parts: from them have been extracted glycerin, explosives, waterproof goods, soaps, and printing ink. Incidentally, they are good to eat, if no more profitable way can be found to consume the crop. On his Chicago Exposition plot Ford laid out one acre for a soy bean exhibit, which comprises, besides growing beans, an old-fashioned barn equipped with a processing plant which groups of small farmers can operate, with a capacity of one third of a ton of beans an hour. Finished moulded parts are being made from a plastic material produced from the residue after extracting the oil.

Growing beans has not interfered with the other aspects of Ford's agricultural experiments. The children of his primary schools cultivate their garden plots, forty by sixty-seven feet each, which are tilled, seeded, and turned over to them, along with small tools made to suit their size and strength. More than 80 per cent of the employees in and around Dearborn spend a part of their time gardening. Men from the smaller factories cultivate larger tracts of their own and share in the co-operative farming on Ford's thousands of acres. The progress of all these undertakings is recorded in the *Ford News,* the company's monthly magazine, along with doings in the plants and agencies. The school-children at Dearborn have their own publication, recently established and entitled the *Herald,* after the newspaper which Edison published in his boyhood.

Holding no official post in his own company, of which his son is the president, Ford presides over his schools, farms, factories, and museum collections. He looks with natural pride upon the vast organization he has built. He likes to wander in the labyrinth of machinery at River Rouge. Doubtless he congratulates himself on having evolved an institution of such immensity. But his thoughts often dwell on a future in which manufacturing will be decentralized and the large factory forced to yield to a system of smaller units closely linked with farm life. As he nears his seventy-second birthday, he has lost none of his faith in change —for the better.

"Are we coming back?" a visitor asked him as the summer of 1934 was approaching, when nearly everybody was still debating whether business recovery was a reality or a mirage.

EDSEL FORD
President of the Ford Motor Company.

"We never come back," he replied. "The saying that history repeats itself has no truth in it. We shall see better times, but never again the same old times."

VIII
DEARBORN, THE WONDER TOWN

DEARBORN, center of the Ford activities, has come
to be a show place unique in the world; it would be a
unrivaled show place if every vestige of manufacturin
business were moved away tomorrow—the Laboratory
the River Rouge Plant, the Airport, and all the othe
buildings identified with the motor industry. For with
out factories Dearborn would still have the Edison In
stitute, which is the name of the combined Ediso
Museum and the Greenfield Village, constructed to en
dure for generations as exhibitions of progress i
engineering, mechanics, and the useful arts and craft

"Hobbies" is a misnomer for these pursuits of Henry
Ford, as each of them has behind it an educational, cultural, or scientific motive. Yet the boyish delight with
which he pours fortunes into enterprises having no
chance of profit, except the satisfaction of seeing them
through, causes a visitor at Dearborn to wonder if there
ever was a pleasure-seeker so lavish or so successful in
discovering the joy of living. His recreations are almost
wholly confined to his business, his exhibitions and
schools and farms, and his laboratory, where he dons
overalls and works on new appliances when the humor
strikes him. Skating is the only sport in which he has
been known to indulge.

Into the museum and historical village, planned to

cover more than two hundred acres, visitors flock from far and near, each paying a quarter of a dollar to see treasures of which no Midas or Maharajah has dreamed. The twenty-five-cent admission fee, by the way, pays about 5 per cent of the cost of showing the visitor around and is designed merely to restrict attendance to

FAÇADE OF REPLICAS AT THE EDISON INSTITUTE
Beyond this historical group of buildings is the vast museum.

those who are interested. In the current year, three or four hundred thousand quarters may be collected at the gates. But the most fantastic estimate of attendance over a lifetime could not pay for the exhibits. Some day, when everybody knows about Dearborn, maybe the ticket-buyers will form an army big enough to defray the incidental expenses of maintaining the vast show.

Imagine a group of buildings which are exact reproductions of Independence Hall, Congress Hall, and the old City Hall of Philadelphia. That is what the visitor sees as he motors a quarter-mile from the Dearborn Inn, the modernized New England hostelry which Ford has built as a model hotel and leased to an operating company. The clock on the tower of Independence Hall chimes the hours. A continual stream of cars passes in and out of the semi-circular driveway. Toward the left side of the group of buildings is the auditorium, an up-to-date theater; to the right, classrooms used by the model school, one of many such institutions established for children living near Ford factories. The museum is in the rear of this façade of architectural replicas.

Much has been said and written about the Edison Institute Museum. Yet nobody can have any conception of its vastness until he goes into it. Miles and miles of space, only partly filled now, stretch out before the astonished newcomer, who soon realizes it would require months, even years, to absorb the knowledge represented by the collections.

If the Madison Square Garden or the Waldorf-Astoria Hotel of New York could be lifted and set down in the museum, neither would cover half of the floor expanse; nor would the Coliseum of Chicago. The vast area, measuring 800 by 440 feet, still far from filled, is already a labyrinth of machinery, vehicles, railway tracks, streets, and miscellaneous inventions that tell the story of the centuries. Over the floor a covering of teakwood is being laid, and the forests of Burma could not send teakwood fast enough to keep pace with the experts employed by Ford to put the strips in place. This hard wood was selected because of its imperviousness to water and rust. Its polished surface glistens like a dancing floor, over which ten thousand couples could waltz without touching elbows. The material for this floor cost about seventy thousand dollars, exclusive of labor. The value of the flooring is mentioned here only to give an idea of the scale on which the museum is being outfitted. Ford and his helpers do not talk about costs in connection with the vast educational plan.

The Dearborn Inn.

Figures would be superfluous, anyway. The pricelessness of the museum's contents, as well as its usefulness, is evident to any casual observer.

There is no limit to the character of inventions or appliances exhibited, nor their dates, nor the countries of their origin. Whatever depicts an advance in science or handicraft, or represents a phase in the development of engineering and mechanics and the useful arts of civilization, has its niche in the exhibition. Every piece of machinery, every table or chair, is renovated until it is as nearly as possible the same usable article it was in the beginning. As fast as the repair shop can do the job, an engine or motor is put into shape for actual running; each machine is able, if reconstruction is possible, to perform the function for which it was built. If Henry Ford wishes to drive a locomotive of 1850 along the rails laid in grooves across the teakwood floor, the clumsy-looking creation can get up steam and go snorting from one side of the building to another; if he chooses to take a reminiscent spin in one of the runabouts built in the 'nineties, all he needs is a gallon of gasoline before he seizes the tiller and dashes over the highway of teak.

So many new impressions crowd themselves into the visitor's consciousness that he is overcome with the futility of trying to grasp all the facts poured into his ear by a clever young guide. Of one thing he is convinced immediately: Ford's chief interest in founding the museum may have been educational and scientific, but there is enough pure entertainment to thrill even a frivolous guest. You may go in search of knowledge, but you will find diversion as well. Or you may reverse the program and go seeking pleasure, only to find that you are being educated in spite of yourself.

Let one stranger, who was overcome by the immensity of the place and the variety of its contents, recall at random a few of the things he saw: the earliest handloom, renovated to look and operate as it did two hundred years ago in Holland. An aisle of ancient spinning wheels, scores of them. Tablefuls of flatirons, all shapes and sizes, flanked by a group of ruffle irons. Pianos enough to fill a Fifth Avenue store. Furniture galore, from Chippendale and Heppelwhite and Hitchcock chairs to horsehair sofas; cabinets, bookcases, highboys, lowboys, beds, every conceivable appurtenance of the household, showing what our ancestors' homes were like fifty or a hundred years ago. A whole street of stores, looking as they did in a village of our great-grandfathers' time, their shelves and walls made of the self-same wood or of modern planks stained and shaped into identical imitations. Shops of a pottery worker, a tinsmith, a candlemaker, a gunsmith, a locksmith, and a harness maker. A volunteer fire department. An apothecary and barber shop. A clothing store of Revolutionary days, filled with the garments men and women wore then. A country hardware store, with all its old pans and pots, the iron stove and worn benches. Musical instruments without count, apropos of which it is said that in the beginning Ford was interested only in their scientific and mechanical attributes, but that of late he is fascinated by their notes as well.

Among the largest exhibits are a marine steam engine, such as was used on transatlantic liners before turbines came, and a generator as big as a house, run by gasoline and steam, which was in the Highland Park plant before the Ford factories were overhauled and rehabilitated in 1927. The mammoth engine—mother of 15,000,000 Fords—is also there. From these mammoths the engines range down to the smallest mechanical contrivances. The history of steam power development is shown from the beginning. An engine of 1760 is the earliest, and there is every type between that and the Highland Park monster.

As would be expected, the display of motor vehicles occupies a large section. Here are all the Ford models except the one treasure too precious even for a well-guarded museum: the first gasoline buggy of 1893, which the inventor keeps in Greenfield Village. There are cars, too, of other makes, American and foreign. No shape or style is lacking. The primitives are there, with small wire wheels, doors at the back, lofty rear seats, bicycle tires, acetylene lamps, and none of the refinements we consider necessary today; the elaborately decorated, enormous affairs of a later decade; cars with one headlight instead of two, with three wheels instead of four, with every eccentric accessory that had its short day and faded out of memory; cars of all colors, length, and heights, with all sorts of engines, brakes, tops, and fittings. Near by are the resurrected "bikes" of the 'eighties and 'nineties, as various in appearance and attachments as were the early automobiles; and the motorcycles of many designs.

Of the more recent relics, the most conspicuous is a Mercedes car which the German Kaiser used in the World War for dashing around from one battlefront to another. It looks old-fashioned now, but is a gorgeous coach, inlaid with fine woods and ivory and gilt, its seats luxuriously upholstered to suit the taste of the War Lord.

One of the features of the transportation group is a reproduction of the *Rocket*, the first successful steam locomotive, constructed in England in 1829. The original drawings were used for this second *Rocket*. A train of cars, their sides decorated with pictures in gay colors and drawn by the historic Sam Hill locomotive, suggests the very style of train from which Edison was ejected as a boy, when an explosion disclosed the fact that the future Wizard of Electricity had a laboratory

concealed in the baggage car. Edison rode in this train
and sold papers to a distinguished company on the
Fiftieth Anniversary of the Invention of the Incandescent Light, observed at Dearborn in October, 1929.

The era of horse-drawn vehicles is recalled by an

IN THE EDISON MUSEUM
*Where railway tracks are imbedded in the famous teakwood
floor.*

array of equipages hardly less extensive than the automobiles. One sees a three-wheeled phaeton in which
General Lafayette rode, a sleigh that carried George
Washington, buggies, racing gigs on two wheels,
coaches, shays, barouches, victorias, buckboards, omni-
buses, wagons, ancient carts, and a still more ancient
Russian vehicle whose two wheels look indestructible.

Many of the old machines and furnishings are not
merely types, but have romantic stories connected with

them. A chandelier has been rescued from some historic building torn down a score of years ago. A mahogany couch was once owned by George Washington. The parlor furniture of Abraham Lincoln, sold by his widow to a family that moved to Canada, and finally redeemed by Ford, occupies a prominent place. Near it is a desk of General Grant. The wood carver's art and the dainty skill of the expert who made early American chairs and tables are shown by examples mended and repolished until they are as good as new.

In the agricultural collection, extending across the building at one end, every kind of farm equipment is shown, from hoes and axes to the threshing machine, including mowers, rakes, plows, beehives, sap buckets, and a multitude of devices both primitive and modern. The blacksmith shop of Caleb Taft, dating back to 1830, has been reproduced entire, and Ford brought its complete equipment from Uxbridge, Mass. An old sling for shoeing oxen, a hand bellows, a forge and various tools are arranged just as they were when the poet Longfellow used to visit his friend the blacksmith.

Ford buys more rapidly than he can have his purchases repaired and arranged. In various odd corners are stored objects of rare interest, awaiting their turn in the renovation shop. The founder's own testing laboratory, in the building where he makes his headquarters, is decorated by a line of chandeliers and lamps a hundred yards in length, because there is not yet a place prepared for them in the museum. All the buildings roundabout are temporarily sheltering exhibits not yet finally rehabilitated. Out in a vacant lot are hundreds of old engines, wheels, and machines, rusty and seemingly

ANTIQUE IMPLEMENTS IN THE MUSEUM
"The Village Smithy," where the poet Longfellow visited his friend Caleb Taft.

abandoned to the elements, which some day will be refurbished and installed where they can teach their lessons of a bygone day.

As the collections grow, so does the library of volumes dealing with scientific subjects in many languages. The books are in rather a jumble now. They are shoved away in several upstairs rooms in one of the Institute's buildings, waiting for an expert librarian to catalogue them and prepare indexes. Meanwhile a young graduate of the Ford Trade School, after making a study of the museum, has been promoted to the job of cataloguing all the articles in the institution. He is one of the Ford organization's enthusiasts. Probably he will not be a young man when his task is finished, but one gets the impression that he thinks the museum is worth all the years anybody can give to it.

The Greenfield Village, like the museum, is dominated by the name of Edison. It was opened to the public on June 13, 1933, after so many Dearborn visitors had asked to see it that a regular schedule was necessary to take care of them. The village is really another museum, with many small buildings gathered around an old-fashioned greensward. No motorcar enters its gates. The first sight that attracts the newcomer's attention is a leisurely procession of wheeled vehicles, each drawn by two horses of quality. In these dignified transports the visitors are taken from one building to another, when the distances are too great for walking. Nearly every aspect of the enclosure reflects village life in America fifty or seventy-five years ago; but a concession to modernity will be a system of hard surfaced highways, because on rainy days the present roads produce some genuine old-fashioned mud.

A tour of the village, under the leadership of a guide trained in the lore of community life in the nineteenth century, begins with a visit to the Clinton Inn. Built in 1831–32, this old hostelry stood in Clinton, Mich., and

Only horses and carriages are used at the Greenfield Village.

was a stopping place for coaches between Detroit and Chicago. Its ballroom has a spring floor, which gives gently under dancing feet. Ford moved the structure intact to Dearborn and has furnished it as it was when a famous ball was held on the spring floor on New Year's Eve of 1876. Hard by is a stone mill, recently completed. The Chapel of Martha-Mary, named for the mothers of Mr. and Mrs. Ford, has a spire modeled after one in Bradford, Mass., and the bricks and front door are from the girlhood home of Mrs. Ford, in Green-field Township, which adjoins her husband's native Dearborn Township. In sight of the inn and the chapel is a stern-paddle Mississippi River boat, floating placidly in the shallows of the River Rouge, which bends around a corner of the village. Ford has installed the original engines in the craft, having bought it in Florida after learning that Edison used to be among its passengers on the Caloosahatchee River.

The original red schoolhouse in which Ford occupied a back seat as a boy, with its desks in replica just as they were in the old days of the Scotch settlement of Dear-born, stands not far from the Lincoln courthouse, the two-story walnut structure imported from Logan County, Ill. A fire lighted by Herbert Hoover in 1929 burns perpetually in the same fireplace where Lincoln warmed himself before addressing the judge.

The Town Hall, community center of the village, faces the common, opposite the chapel. Across the street is the ornamental jewelry shop of Sir John Bennett, celebrated watchmaker of Fleet Street, London, im-ported intact with its clock tower and its effigies of Gog and Magog over the doorway. Inside are glass cases filled with watches and other examples of the jeweler's art, and massive clocks ranging from the fancy French type to a great gilded timepiece built in the form of an Oriental palace for an Indian potentate. The collection of watches has a particular sentimental value for Ford, who in his younger days was hesitant between the two ambitions of making horseless vehicles and manufac-turing watches.

A rectangular yard, with a white picket fence around it, contains the preëminent exhibit of the village—the Menlo Park group of buildings, reconstructed from, or reproductions of, the structures in which Thomas A. Edison labored from 1876 to 1886. From New Jersey, too, was brought Francis Jehl. No fairy tale can rival the story of Mr. Jehl, who presides over the identical laboratory in which he worked with Edison as the chief assistant of the inventor. He is the only man in all the world who ever recaptured his youth. Sitting there in the Menlo Park Laboratory, surrounded by the early models of the incandescent light, the first phonograph, the original carbon telephone transmitter, and all the incidental equipment of Edison's workshop, Francis Jehl gives the lie to the fact that time cannot turn back; for him it is actually repeating itself. When he shows you his treasures (for they seem to belong to him quite as much as to Henry Ford), you have the feeling that he imagines his former chief is still standing at his elbow. He talks of Edison as though the great inventor were present in the flesh, while he caresses an incandescent bulb within which a yellow light shines from the original filament made of carbonized paper, or shows how the first mimeograph is operated, or demonstrates the working of the earliest Edison telephone. If there is a happier human than Jehl, this chronicler has not seen him.

In one corner of the laboratory stands the telegraph table at which Edison sat and talked with his fingers to distant friends before the telephone was invented. He used the table first in Newark, then Menlo Park, West

Orange, and Fort Myers, Fla. It followed him through life until he gave it to Ford.

The armchair used by the Wizard as he experimented with incandescent lamps stands close by. From that chair for forty hours he watched his final test on October 21, 1879. When this moment was reënacted on its fiftieth anniversary, he sat in the chair again, while President Hoover and Mr. Ford stood behind him. On a stepladder, operating the mercury pump to exhaust the air from the lamp, was Francis Jehl, now the last survivor of those who assisted Edison in the laboratory during that period. So accurately had the room been restored for the celebration that Edison declared it was 99.9 per cent perfect.

"What about the other one-tenth of one per cent?" asked Ford.

"Oh, look at that floor!" exclaimed Edison. "It is nowhere near so dirty as ours used to be."

The office and library building used by Edison in Menlo Park had been dismantled, so Ford reconstructed it with bricks from the same yard that supplied the material for the original structure. The small carbon shed and carpenter shop, like the larger buildings, are placed in exactly the same relative positions they occupied in New Jersey. In the Edison group are nine structures. The one that most interests the sightseer, after the laboratory, is Mrs. Sarah Jordan's Boarding House, where some of the inventor's helpers took their meals. Wires were run to it for the first successful demonstration of the incandescent lamp as an invention for household use.

Farther along the village streets, after leaving the

Edison section, the visitor enters Luther Burbank's office, transported from his experimental farm in California, and next the restored Canadian homestead of Edison's father, who fled to the United States after he was accused of complicity in the rebellion of 1837. The Cotswold Cottage Group, more than two centuries old, imported from England and reconstructed to appear exactly as it was in the sheepherding district where it sheltered two families for ten or twelve generations, has been equipped with furniture of the sixteenth century, including leather pitchers, wooden trenchers, and a Bible chest. The Secretary House, constructed in 1751 at Exeter, N. H., is an example of early Colonial architecture. Clark House, erected by Henry Ford's uncle, was brought to the village as a typical specimen of the homes common to Michigan seventy-five years ago.

One of the smallest cottages is the one in which the late Charles P. Steinmetz, consulting engineer of the General Electric Company, found seclusion in the woods near Schenectady, N. Y. Another diminutive structure is the Greenfield Post Office, built in Connecticut in 1803. On its new site, it is not only a decorative antique, but actually handles Uncle Sam's mails, doing a considerable business in souvenir postcards nowadays. An old pharmacy with its complete stock of bottles and files of old prescriptions occupies one end of the building, which is put together with hand-wrought nails and has hand-made shutters and laths.

Then one visits the Tintype Studio, a relic of days almost forgotten; also the Waterford Country Store, its ante-bellum contents intact, and the Gardner Home, a pioneer house aged one hundred and eleven years.

A log cabin, with an outdoor oven at the back, is an importation from the countryside near Ford's boyhood home. A tiny shoemaking shop has been brought from Massachusetts, where it was built in 1828 as a tollkeeper's stall on the banks of the Merrimac. Next door is a restored house from Plymouth, Mich., dating from 1845. A shoe shop from New Hampshire and a cooperage shop from the same state, the latter built in 1785, are fitting neighbors of a blacksmith's place, the boss of which shoes the fine horses that haul carriages and shays about the village.

One cannot get away from memories of Edison in the village, which includes the old Smith's Creek station where the boy Edison was put off a Grand Trunk train for setting fire to the contents of the baggage car, while he was acting officially as news agent and personally as an amateur chemist. Where the boy and his "laboratory" were ousted from the car, the depot has been restored to its condition of sixty years ago. The old-fashioned luggage, the telegraph instruments and the living quarters of the agent are all there, and a train resembling the one on which Edison sold newspapers and confections stands in the museum. A special track was laid to bring Edison and the other distinguished guests to the half-century anniversary celebration in 1929.

A frame shelter houses the only original Edison jumbo dynamo which was not burned in the Pearl Street electrical station fire of 1890. An old carding mill, erected a century ago, to which the Michigan farmers hauled their wool, is used by the students of Ford's school for weaving cloth in the old patterns. A historical pipe engine house, where volunteer firemen stored their engine and equipment, was brought from New Hampshire, and the first power silk mill built in the United States from Connecticut. A Sandwich glass plant has been reconstructed by using some of the original bricks from America's first pressed glass factory in Cape Cod, Mass. An aged foundry was transported from Lapeer, Michigan; a stone burr grist mill from the River Raisin near Monroe, Mich., and a ninety-year-old sawmill from the same neighborhood.

Many among the historic relics in the village have a sentimental interest for Henry Ford, linked as they are with his own life. He drops into his old workshop almost daily. It is a small brick affair, and it stood in the backyard of his house at 58 Bagley Avenue, Detroit. There he built his first automobile, the gasoline buggy of 1893, while employed as engineer by the Detroit Edison Company. Bringing back recollections of a still earlier time is the reconstructed log cabin in which was born William Holmes McGuffey, whose school readers were used in the classes Ford attended, as they were in thousands of other schoolrooms throughout the land. The cabin was moved from Pennsylvania. A recent acquisition from that state, purchased for renovation on a site beside the McGuffey memorial, is the cottage birthplace of Stephen Collins Foster, composer of some of the most famous of American songs.

The Armington and Sims Machine Shop, a typical steam engine manufacturing plant of the 'eighties, from which Edison bought a high-speed engine for use in his first incandescent lighting system, is another building which Ford often visits. This plant was moved to Dearborn practically intact. Ford lingers over its old machines, discussing their points with the man in charge. The workings of a steam engine are as fascinating to the inventor today as they were when at the age of twelve years he watched a lumbering road machine and dreamed his dreams of the horseless carriage.

Few are the modern touches in the Greenfield Village. When any new thing is permitted to intrude itself into the company of the antiques, there is a practical and educational reason for it, and the incongruity is lost in continuity. The Research Laboratory, wherein students of the Ford school carry on experiments in agricultural chemistry, is an up-to-date workshop in form and equipment. Another such structure is the temporary Soy Bean Extracting Plant, where the experimental farm pupils learn about the famous beans and their by-products, which of late have played so great a part in the making of Ford automobiles.

The inventor's concentration of historic relics at Dearborn, while it represents the major part of his collections, does not tell all the story. He has bought and renovated many other old buildings, distinctive of their periods, and left them on their original sites, notably the Wayside Inn, at South Sudbury, Mass., and the Botsford Inn, sixteen miles from Detroit. In these restorations he has played his part in a national movement. Thirty-five years of the automobile and good roads—from 1895, when only 4 motorcars were registered in the United States, to 1930, when the peak of 23,000,000 cars was reached—saw more than 600 historic buildings in this country opened as public shrines. Similarly, the growth of rapid and comfortable road transport may be credited with the success of our National Parks, whose attractions might as well have been non-existent if the motor had not made them accessible.

The school at the Edison Institute, though it is one of a chain of schools operated in connection with Ford enterprises and is conducted on the same principles as the others in the system, has the distinction of being continually under the personal supervision of the founder. Its 110 pupils, ranging from five to thirteen years old and reaching what is called the "junior high" grade, are recruited from the Dearborn district immediately surrounding Ford headquarters. The applicants are numerous, and each waits his or her turn for admittance. Favoritism is barred. First come, first served, is the rule. At a recent gathering of the children, the daughter of a plant employee and a niece of Mrs. Henry Ford were pointed out as two typical members of the higher classes.

In other Ford schools the children are under expert teachers and occupy scientifically arranged buildings, but only at the Edison Institute are there such facilities for the absorption of knowledge as are afforded by the museum and the historical village. The fairy-tale existence of these young people of Dearborn dazzles one's imagination. As a department head in the organization remarked recently to the writer:

"No small school in the world is maintained at such cost or with such unlimited equipment, and yet the students pay not a cent for tuition."

The comradeship between Henry Ford and the youngsters is illustrative of the manufacturer's interest

Henry Ford and school children, at Greenfield Village.

in activities outside his factories. No day is too busy for him to visit one or another group of the children, some of them busy in classrooms, others learning the lessons of the museum or the village. It is not unusual for him to act as guide, surrounded by boys and girls, among the mechanical wonders of the institute. Love of children is his ruling passion, even throwing into the background, for hours together, his devotion to the motor and the steam engine. The girls and boys take liberties with the museum treasures that would bring an immediate rebuke to any grown-up. It is related that the younger children, when the chief is with them, crawl in and out of locomotive cabs, leap upon antique cars that are usually guarded as too sacred for ordinary mortals

Greenfield Village school children in Pinafore—*Henry Ford as impresario.*

to touch, and even ride bicycles over the teakwood floor.

The grand climax of the school year in 1934 was a musical revue, with Ford as impresario. In the Museum Theatre, as comfortable a playhouse as Broadway can boast, the 110 children put on a part of the operetta *Pinafore*, performed old-fashioned dances (including the waltz, which seems not to be out of style any more), and sang old songs before an audience that packed the house and enjoyed every minute of the show. In the front row of the balcony sat Ford, as happy as the youngest of the players.

After an overture by the Ford orchestra, composed of workers in the plants, and a prologue by two students, came the *Pinafore* scene. In that and the succeeding numbers every pupil had some part; not one of the 110 was left out, from the tiny five-year-olds to the dignified elders of twelve and thirteen years. The Admiral of the Queen's Navee disported himself in gold lace and cocked hat with becoming gravity, and the convolutions of the huge chorus were faultlessly precise. It was evident that there had been expert trainers for all the performers in that show, and no professional producer was ever more careful about the accuracy of his costumes or the brilliance of his scene painting.

Of the miscellaneous musical and dancing numbers, the violin solos of a twelve-year-old boy were of tremendous interest for a very special reason. In the Ford world news travels fast, as it does in less model worlds. Everybody in or about Dearborn knew that the violinist that evening was playing Mr. Ford's Stradivarius valued at $50,000. It must be recorded that the performer acted as naturally as though the treasure in his hands were a five-dollar fiddle.

Some of the songs the boys and girls sang were "My Hero," "I Can't Do That Sum," "When You and I Were Young, Maggie," the Toreador song, and "Because You're You." A modern number was "The Last

THE EXPERIMENTAL LABORATORY, DEARBORN
Here Henry Ford has his headquarters, though rarely occupying his private office.

Round-up." In a long list of dances were included the polka, gallop, reel, and quadrille, besides the waltzes in which many couples circled over the stage with a skill acquired through regular lessons from a dancing master during the past months. In the last part of the program, following a gorgeous scene depicting a gypsy camp, were the Anvil Chorus, a scarf dance, and songs reflecting life in the woodland. When it was all over, a large individual, who had no part in the show and was by no means as gorgeously costumed as the young participants, retrieved the Stradivarius and took it away to a place of safety.

That incident of the priceless violin typifies the story of Henry Ford. Nothing was left undone to make the boy musician's performance as nearly perfect as possible; the best instrument was none too good. It is with the same ardor for perfection that the motor manufacturer still demands change, always change, in the mechanical details of cars and engines. The chief chemist and metallurgist at the River Rouge Plant is confronted with a demand that he reduce the weight of a valve push-rod one seventh of an ounce without affecting its strength. The expert on paint is bidden to improve his soy-bean product to last longer and shine better. So it goes, through all the departments. Tests to improve a single screw or bolt continue for months. The pursuit of the ultimate goal, economical service, has persisted from the inception of the "universal car" to the V-8 with its fifteen thousand parts.